19th Century
LOUISIANA PAINTERS AND PAINTINGS

from the

Collection of W. E. GROVES

Martin and Margaret Wiesendanger
Curators of the Collection

PELICAN PUBLISHING COMPANY
GRETNA 1971

ISBN 0-911116-52-4

Published by PELICAN PUBLISHING COMPANY
630 Burmaster Street, Gretna, Louisiana 70053

Printed in U.S.A.
by LABORDE PRINTING CO.
New Orleans, La.

FOREWORD

Louisiana painting of the nineteenth century, may be said to be story-telling documentary. The age of steam cancelled the Diderot outlook of the eighteenth century, and produced literal subjectivism. So, in the eighteen thirties we have a precise recording of hard core reality, flavored with an exuberant romanticism and seasoned with the delicious shudder of the Gothic novel.

It may further be said of nineteenth century art, that the turned spool wood architecture of the steamboat and the Victorian house, which superseded the classic detailed Strickland, Latrobe, Gallier and Howard style, was indicative of the discovery of the steam lathe and the substitution of steam power for man and animal power. This deliberation induced a euphoric nature into painting. There was a summary carrying out of all effects in nature, portrait or stillife landscape, history and regionalism in two and three-dimensional media.

Then came the daguerrotype. On January 15, 1839, S.F.B. Morse saw Daguerre's exhibit in Paris and wrote modestly, that "the two great wonders exhibited in Paris are the Daguerrotype and Morse's Electro Magnetic Telegraph". In 1839 Daguerre published his invention with full instructions, and D. W. Seager showed his first Daguerrotype in America November 7th of the same year "A View of the Unitarian Church from New York University". Jules Lion is credited with being the first to bring the Daguerrotype machine to New Orleans; he may have been making them as early as 1840, although his first advertisement is in 1842. (See comments on Lion under his name.)

From this time on, the influence of the photograph on painting becomes a factor, particularly in some portraiture. W. A. Walker, the celebrated painter of cotton field labor, uses the camera to capture poses quickly. Toward the end of the 19th century, photography, painting and printmaking formed a more or less sanctimonious alliance, from which art has never quite escaped.

The W. E. Groves Collection contains some fifteen hundred paintings, prints and watercolors, daguerrotypes and miniatures, including one hundred and fifty-five portraits and two hundred and seventeen landscapes pertaining to Louisiana. From these we selected the material in this catalogue. The collection further contains the I. M. Cline library, consisting of photographic and scrapbook material relative to New Orleans, a reference library pertaining to largely American artists, and a voluminous catalogue collection of both auctions and exhibitions. Last we mention the W. E. Groves archives of information relative to a 30 year period of intensive collecting.

Martin Wiesendanger
New Orleans 1971

ACKNOWLEDGMENTS

We wish to express appreciation for permitted access to records granted by Mr. James Byrnes of the Isaac Delgado Museum, New Orleans, and Mrs. Peggy Richards of the Louisiana State Museum: for information supplied by Mr. Jordan, Registrar, Delgado Museum; Mr. Harter of the Curatorial Staff, Louisiana State Museum; Mrs. Oalman of the Library at Jackson Barracks, New Orleans; Mr. Hamer, City Archivist, New Orleans Public Library; and to Mr. Collison of the Howard Tilton Library, Tulane University: for particulars on the lives of Artists, to Mrs. Ben C. Toledano on W. A. Walker; to Mr. Toledano and Mr. J. Bernard on Alfred Toledano; to Mrs. Ken Broadwell and Miss Alice Viavant on G. J. Viavant; to Mrs. Marcia Mayfield Matthews, and Miss Sally Mayfield on R. P. Mayfield; to Mr. J. Ben Meyer on the history of his house; to Mr. C. W. Boyle on his father; to Mr. and Mrs. L. Williams on Blanche Blanchard; to Miss Linda Orr on Bernard; and to Mr. Carol Bowers, Mrs. Phyllis Hudson and Mr. Ray Samuel, for miscellaneous information.

Mr. W. E. Groves' notes, now in the Archives of the Collection, proved indispensable. He wishes appreciation expressed to the many people over the years who have supplied him with data.

Martin and Margaret Wiesendanger
New Orleans 1971

NOTES ON COLLECTING

by W. E. GROVES

Collecting is a vice that brooks no competition from other vices. It is a passion that grows and dominates until you stand trembling before the object of your desire, determined to own it at all costs while earnestly striving to conceal your cupidity lest it affect the price.

I fell into the collecting habit quite innocently. Having rented a house in the uptown section of New Orleans, I found that the dining room had a narrow shelf around the wall some six and one-half or seven feet off the floor. Upon inquiring, I was told this was a "plate rail" used for displaying decorative china.

I liked the idea and thought to incorporate it in a house I was building at the time, but my wife and the contractor talked me out of it and substituted two cabinets with oval tops, one on either side of the door between the dining room and the kitchen, which they insisted would do just as well and be more practical.

As the house neared completion, I began the search for antique china to display in the cabinets. After acquiring several pieces, someone on Royal Street suggested I see Dr. I. M. Cline, the former weatherman who had retired and ran a small shop on St. Peter Street. I called on him during one of my lunch hour collecting tours and immediately was treated to a lecture on using antique glass rather than china. The acquaintance broadened into daily noon hour visits and eventually week-end visits as well and I became a collector of glass — in depth.

Dr. Cline, famous as an early weatherman and as developer of a theory regarding the path of hurricanes, before the plane watchers took over, was also noted as a collector of glass and oil paintings. As our friendship developed, he continually urged me to add the collection of paintings to my hobby but I resisted, arguing that the glass could be used for decoration in my home, but paintings would soon become a storage problem. Even then I must have foreseen the extent of my weakness and made feeble efforts to avoid falling a victim.

Eventually, I was persuaded to buy one painting, a large portrait of a Creole lady by an unknown artist, which Dr. Cline agreed to clean and varnish as a surprise Christmas present for my wife. As the cleaning progressed, I became more and more disturbed about the size of the painting and whether it could be hung in my small house. I finally expressed my fears to Dr. Cline who immediately offered to substitute a small painting of a woman by Lansot. I accepted the substitution but doubt kept gnawing at me and finally I decided to take both paintings. Then, there was a large painting of a child signed "Thorpe" which had come from the same house as the Creole lady and could hardly be separated from her — and so I fell.

Fortunately, Dr. Cline had a large attic space on his third floor, and we stored the paintings there. Not having much money, I entered into an arrangement whereby we put the paintings in the attic and I paid fifty dollars per month on an account kept by the good doctor. This led eventually to his automatically acquiring paintings he thought I should have and adding them to my bill. Some of the finest things I have ever owned came from Dr. Cline's interest and advice in my collecting. Of course, I began to hunt on the side and occasionally would find that I was bidding against myself at an auction where, unbeknownst to me, Dr. Cline also had an agent.

I remember Dr. Cline insisting that I purchase an old painting which had been taken off the stretcher and thrown over the back of a chair. The painting was that of a man done in what appeared to be house paint and signed on the back "Bingham". It was wrinkled and had a hole in it and Dr. Cline insisted that I buy it for five dollars because "Bingham" (George Caleb Bingham) was listed in the books as a famous painter of Mississippi River scenes. It required several visits and much argument before I made the investment.

Collecting has been a way of life for me now for more than thirty years and I can truthfully say that I have enjoyed it immensely. There are so many pleasant memories connected with the seeking out and finding of these paintings, many of which would have been destroyed had I not collected and preserved them.

The greatest source of the satisfaction which has come as a result of my hobby are the many friends I made along the way who have helped me in finding and acquiring the bits of history which make up the collection.

None of this would have been possible had these people not taken an interest in the collection and given me much valuable assistance.

While there are so many people involved, it would be impossible to thank all of them, I think that mention should be made here of some of those who made the greatest contribution.

First of all, of course, this book would not be possible had not Margaret and Martin Wiesendanger contributed so much of their time and know-how, first to the indexing and cataloguing of the collection and then to the actual preparation of the book. While the collection was mine, it can truly be said that the book is theirs, as they did the work.

In my collecting I have been helped immeasurably by many people, some of whom are now dead. I have already mentioned Dr. Cline, who started me collecting and who gave me the advantage of his experience and guidance through all of my early days in this field. Carol Bowers and Fernand Sanchez were two dealers who furnished me with some of the finest items in the collection. Walter Goldstein did a great deal of research on the directories of the City of New Orleans and furnished me with a list of artists appearing in many of them.

A further list of people who have helped me would sound like a roster of all of the dealers in antiques in the City of New Orleans, both living and dead. I would like to take this opportunity to thank all of them.

506 Frenchmen St.
New Orleans, La.
April, 1971

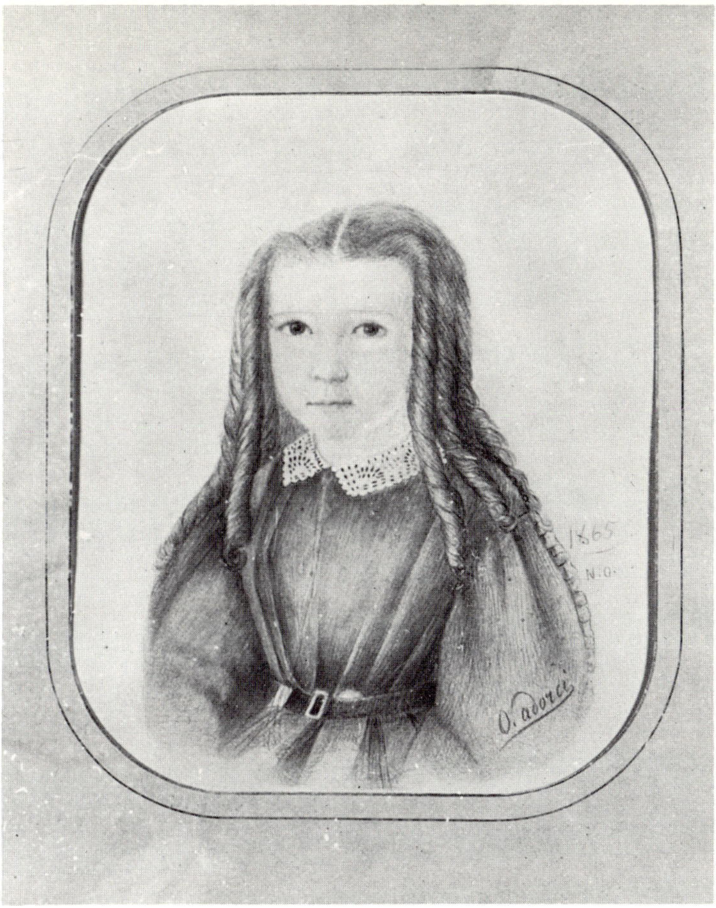

ADORCI, OCTAVE
Drawing of young girl
14" x 6"

signed "1865 N.O.
O. adorci"

Adorci, Octave

Listed in the 1867 New Orleans directory as a portrait painter. The date on the above drawing shows him to have been in New Orleans two years earlier.

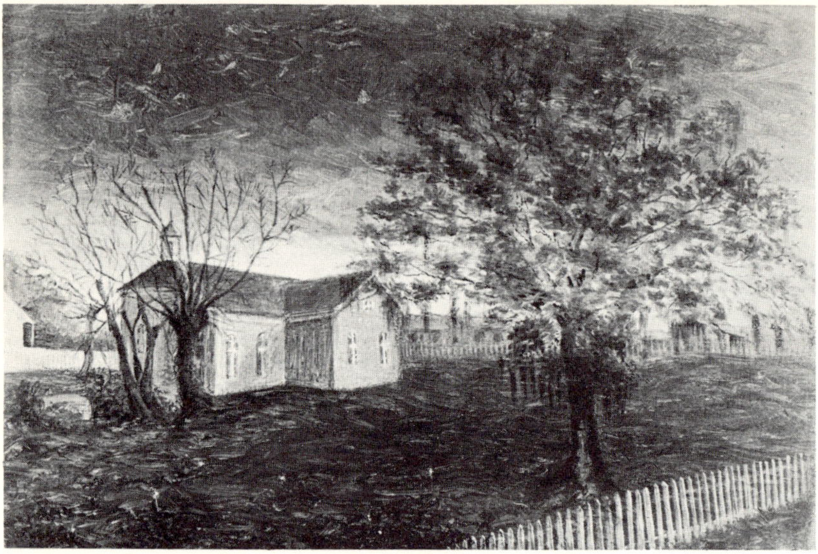

ALAUX, ALEXANDER (signed)
Churchyard
Oil on canvas 11" x 15"

Alaux, Alexander, 1851-1932

Came to Louisiana from Lorraine Province, France, as a child or young man. Studied with Bernard, Ciceri and Philastri in New Orleans, then at the Ecole des Beaus Arts in Brussels. As well as original works, he did many copies of early portraits important in the history of New Orleans. Those in miniature are of especially fine workmanship (see La. State Museum collection).

Alaux's daughter, Marie, is also represented in the collection.

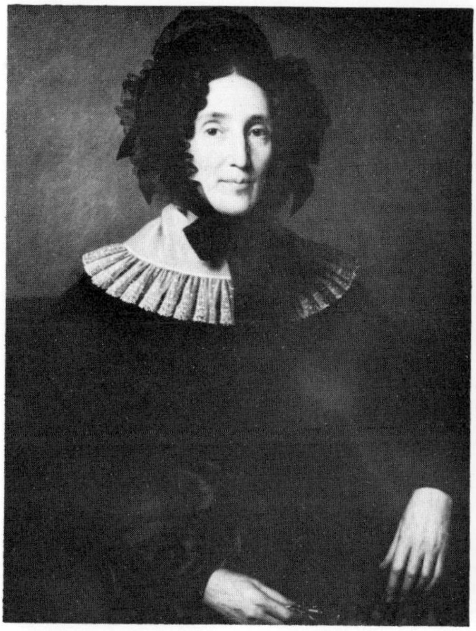

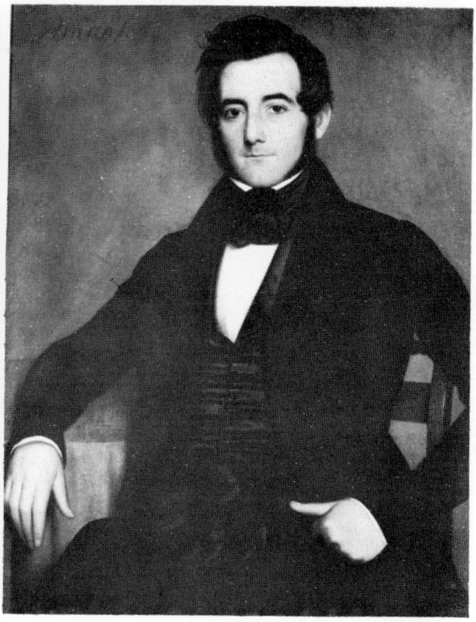

AMANS, JAQUES
Portrait of woman 36" x 29"
Courtesy the Anglo-American Museum
Baton Rouge, Louisiana
Gift of Mr. and Mrs. William E. Groves

(signed)
Portrait of man "36 x 29"
Courtesy Hays Town
Baton Rouge
formerly in the Groves Collection

Amans, Jaques (born 1801, died in Paris, 1888)

Listed in Benezit, oddly enough, as American School, exhibiting many times in Paris between 1831 and 1837. However, he died in Paris, was certainly trained in France, as Coulon speaks of him as coming to New Orleans as a portrait painter. Fielding lists him as painting portraits in New Orleans between 1828 and 1856. The directory shows him at 163 Royal Street in 1838, at 184 Royal in 1840, and at Bienville and Customhouse Streets 1854-56.

Amans ranks as one of the truly technically accomplished painters working in New Orleans. His portraits are straightforward likenesses, with less flamboyancy or romanticizing than his contemporaries. He paints with a full brush and muted tonalities, the flesh tones tending toward ivory, never ruddy. The chief clue toward recognition of his work is the delicate rainbow halftones in the skin shading, the prismatic effect being particularly noticeable at the hairline.

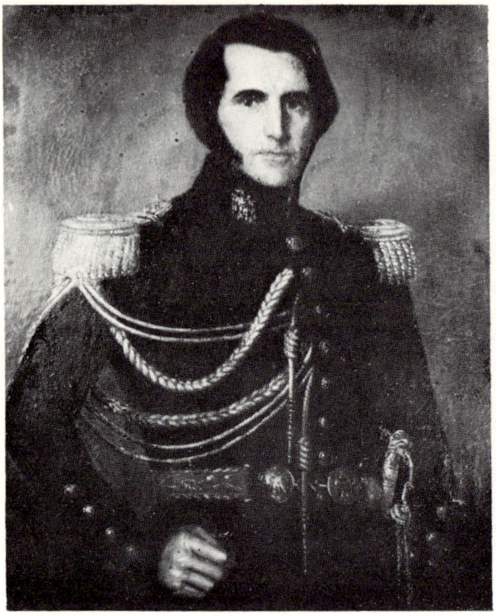

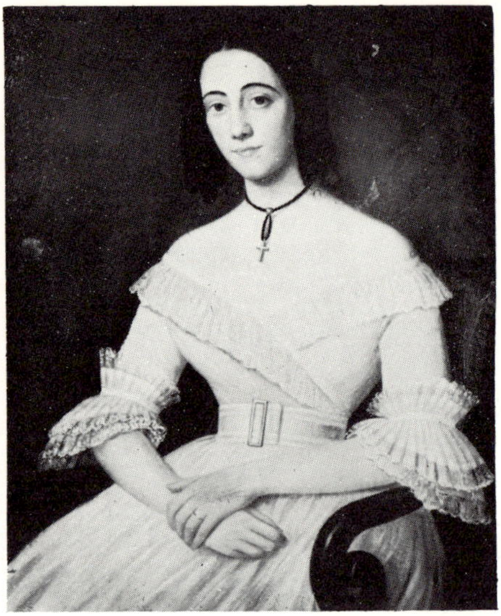

AMANS, JACQUES
Portraits of Prince Murat and his wife
oil on canvas, 36" x 29"

(signed "Amans")

Napoleon Achille Murat (1801-1847), son of Joachim Murat, brilliant cavalry general under Napoleon, and of Caroline Bonaparte, younger sister of the consul, emigrated to Florida in 1821, where he settled near Tallahassee, serving as postmaster 1821-38. He married a grand-niece of Washington, and published a volume of his letters and two books about American politics.

He is sometimes erroneously stated as living in Baton Rouge, but apparently he did have a house at Pearl River, La., and is known to have been a frequent visitor in New Orleans, so that it was natural for him to have portraits painted by Amans, who is not known to have worked outside of New Orleans in this country.

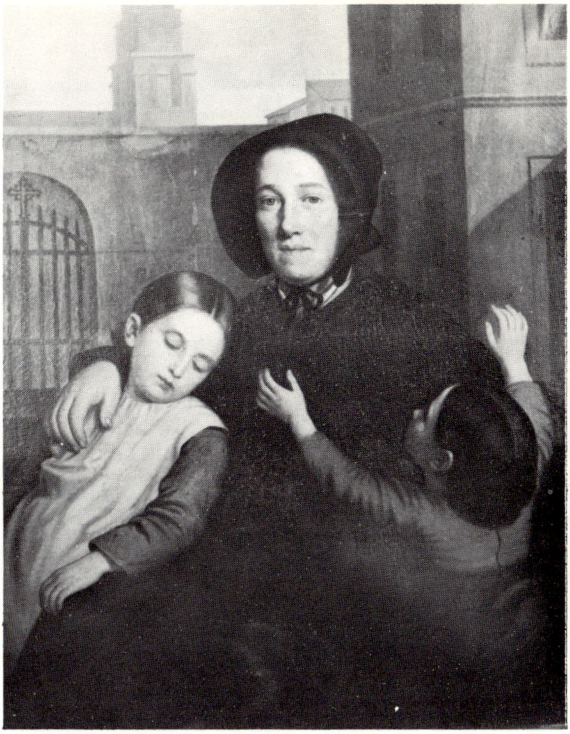

AMANS, JAQUES (signed)
"Margaret"
oil on canvas, 45" x 36"

When the Sisters of Charity in New Orleans were wondering where they were going to get the money to build the orphanage they felt was badly needed, there came to them a laundress working at the St. Charles Hotel. Orphaned as a child herself, she had since lost her husband and only child. She offered all of her meagre savings and two-thirds of her weekly earnings to the sisters to start the orphanage, and devoted the rest of her life to making money to support this orphanage and to help in the building of the larger St. Vincent's Infant Asylum ("my baby house", she called it) and the Elizabeth Asylum for older girls.

This remarkable woman, whose name was Margaret Haughery, built a large dairy business starting with two cows and a dairy cart, and later operated a bakery and bakers' cart, the bakery having been accepted in payment of a debt. When she died, she was such a familiar and well-loved figure in her calico dress and sunbonnet that a statue was erected to her memory, still standing.

Amans has painted her with the tower of the Church of St. Teresa of Avila in the background. The painting was first exhibited in 1851.

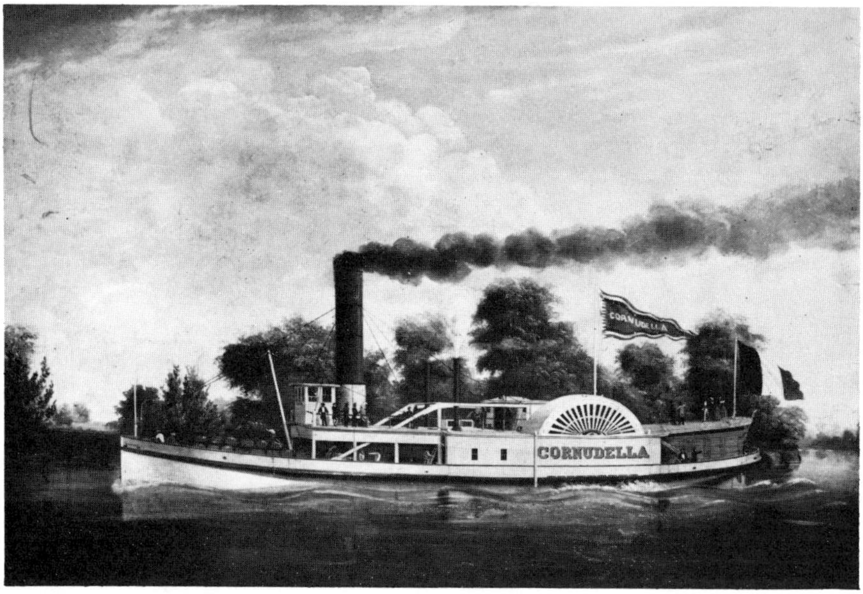

ARNOLD, EDWARD (signed)
The Cornudella
oil on canvas, 22" x 30"

Arnold, Edward (born 1824, died in New Orleans 1866)

First listed in the New Orleans directory of 1853, but came to the city some years earlier. He was a fine marine painter, and most of his known works are Louisiana coastal, lake and river scenes, with emphasis on the ships sailing these waters. The "Cornudella" shown above carries a Mexican flag. It has been surmised that it is a ship running the blockade during the Civil War.

Arnold is listed at 7 Mandeville 1853-4, at 66 Louisa in '55 and '56, after that living at 74 Mandeville with a studio at Royal and Bienville. Several of his paintings are signed Evans and Arnold. **J. G. Evans** (active c. 1840-59) was a marine and historical painter; he worked with Arnold in New Orleans in 1850.

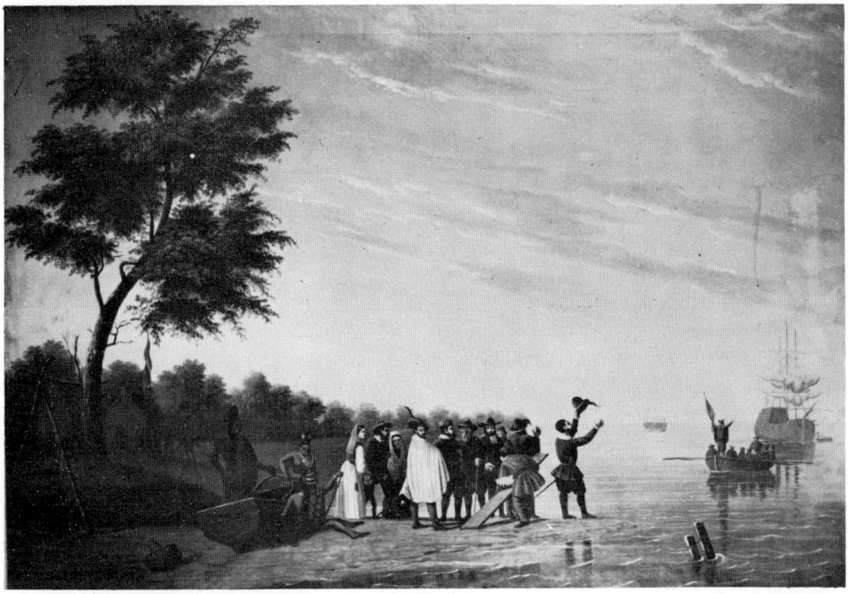

ARNOLD, EDWARD (after Chapman) (signed)
The Landing at Jamestown
oil on canvas, 29" x 30"

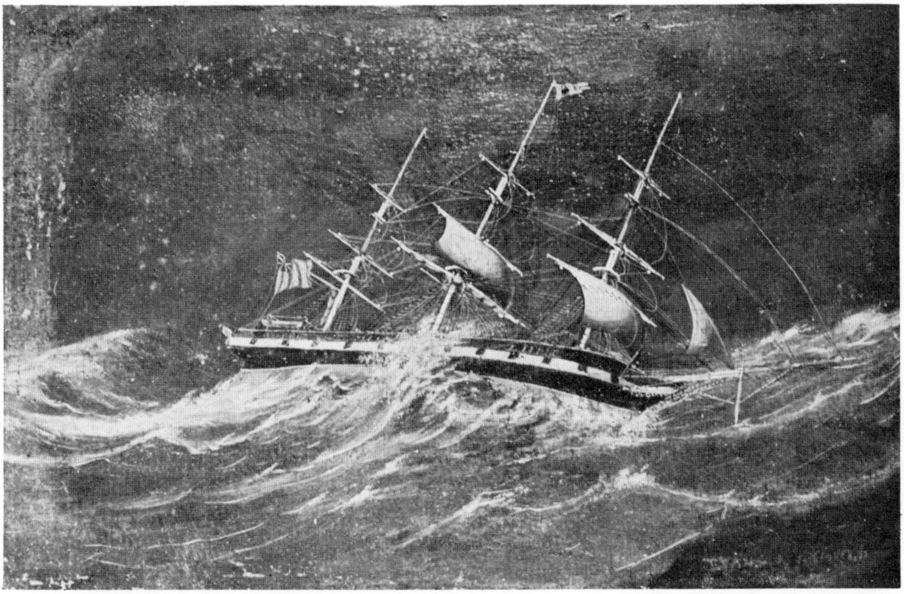

ARNOLD, EDWARD, and EVANS, J. D. signed, Evans and Arnold
British Ship in a storm
oil on canvas, 16" x 23¾"

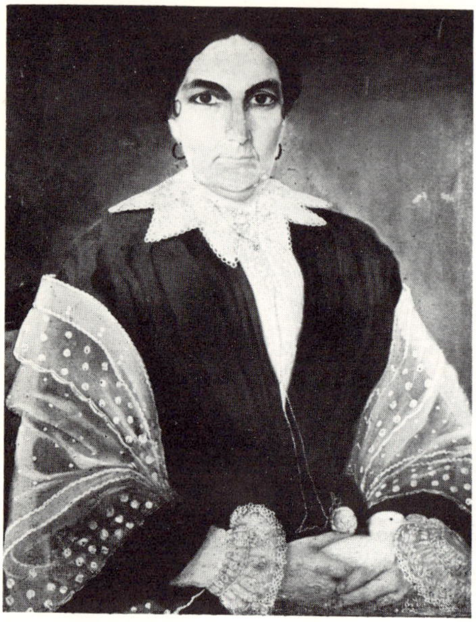

AUDUBON, JOHN J. (signed J.J.A.)
Portrait of Lucy Bakewell Audubon
30" x 25"

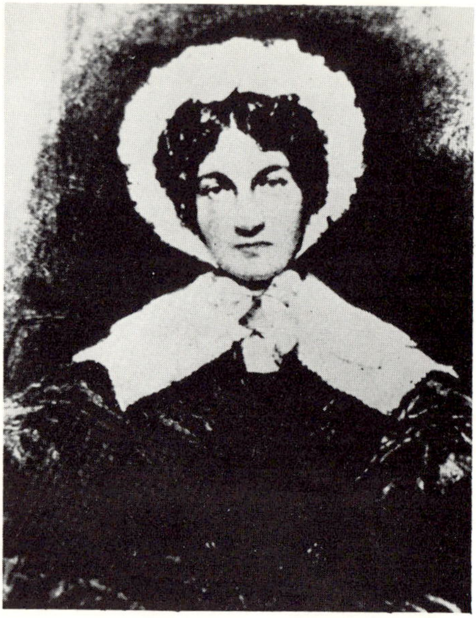

Portrait of Lucy Bakewell Audubon
Miniature on ivory by Frederick
Cruikshank
London 1831

Audubon, John J., 1785-1851

Painter, dancing master, dead shot, naturalist and egotist, arrived in the United States in 1806 and made the great contribution to American ornithology in life-size drawings. On March 29th in 1821 at New Orleans, he shot and drew the White Heron.

In 1822 he was teaching at Washington, Mississippi at Elizabeth Academy. In December he met the artist John Steen from Washington, Pa., who taught him the technique of oil painting. Audubon's birds were drawn in watercolor and his bread and butter portraits in conte crayon. The first oil was an otter from one of his watercolors, the second, the large painting of Natchez, first hung in the Profilet store at Natchez, then sent to France where it was cut down to its present size, returned to Natchez, purchased by Mr. Kelly of Melrose Plantation, Natchez, where it hangs today.

The portraits of his sons, Victor and John Wodehouse, a self-portrait, and the above newly-discovered portrait of his wife are of this same period. The painting of Lucy is modelled allaprima on the "window shade canvas" with some impasto in the lace of the dress. Pigments are lead white, with cinnabar, yellow ochre, and a slight touch of Scheel's Green in the fleshtones with a rose madder glaze. The blue of the dress seems to be basic Prussian blue with an admixture of indigo. The reds are mercuric sulphide or vermilion.

Lucy, who tutored in Natchez, and helped finance his trip to Europe to get his "Birds of America" published, even shared his interest enough to be painted holding a young egret. Audubon has painted her with the birdlike expression so common in his portraits (see his self-portrait, now in the Rinehart Collection, made at Beechwood, Feliciana Parish, in 1822, fontispiece in S. C. Arthur's "Audubon, an Intimate Life of the American Woodsman").

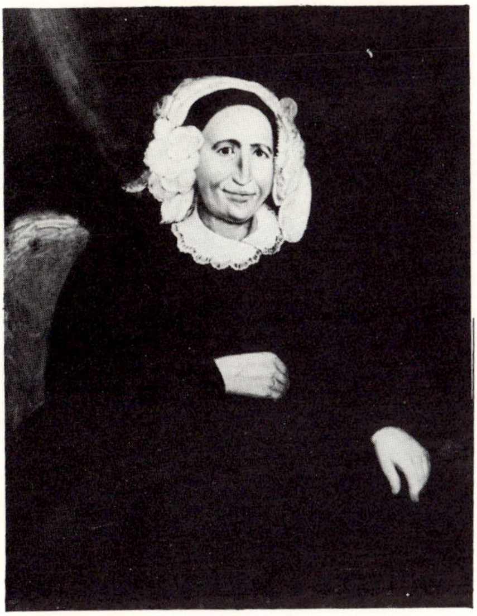

BAKER, WILLIAM H.
Portrait of woman (probably a member of the family of Louisiana Governor Wells), 36" x 29", not signed, but has part of a business card glued to the canvas, reading "W. H. . . . PORTR . . . corner Can . . . UPSTAIRS"

Baker, William H., 1825-1875

According to Cline's notes was "brought up in mercantile pursuits in New Orleans", devoting his spare time to the study of art. He had a studio at 123 Canal St. from 1853 to 1861 and was professionally active as a portrait painter and teacher from about 1850 on. He had been north before 1854, and for some years previous to 1858 was spending only winter and spring in New Orleans, the rest of the time in New York, or possibly Brooklyn, where he settled permanently, serving as principal of the Brooklyn Art Association from 1869 till his death in 1875.

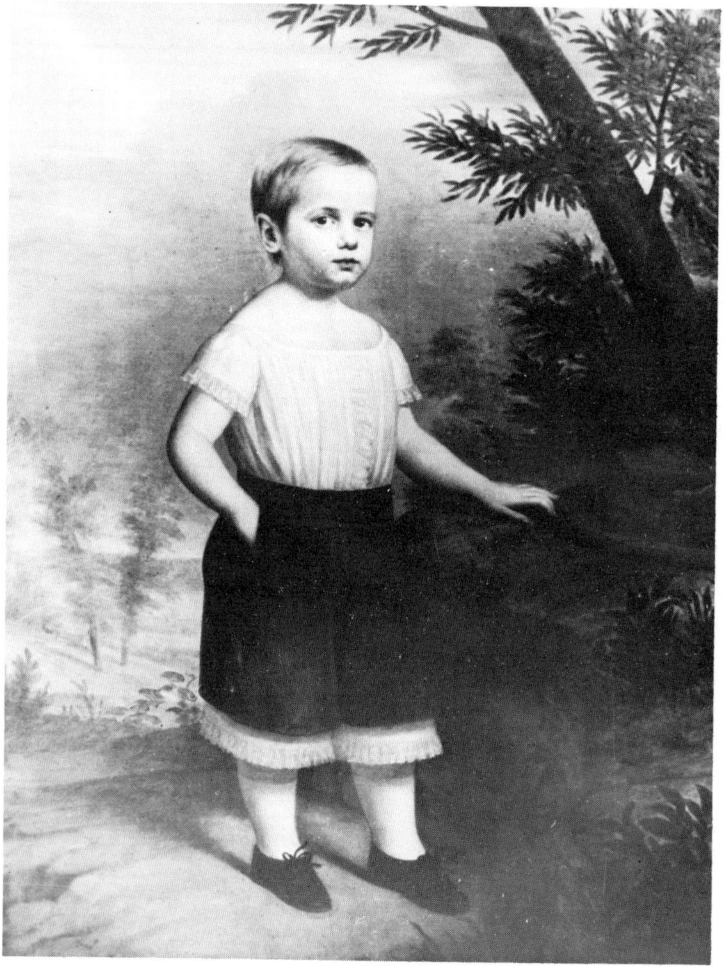

BERNARD, FRANCISCO
Portrait of Boy
46" x 35"

(signed, "Bernard")

Bernard, Francisco (dates unknown)

Records show Bernard to have been painting in New Orleans in the years from 1856 to 1860 and "returning" in 1867. One portrait in the W. E. Groves Collection is dated 1870. Examples of his work have been found in New Jersey, and many exist in New Orleans in museum and private collections, including some fine pastel portraits preserved by relatives of the sitters.

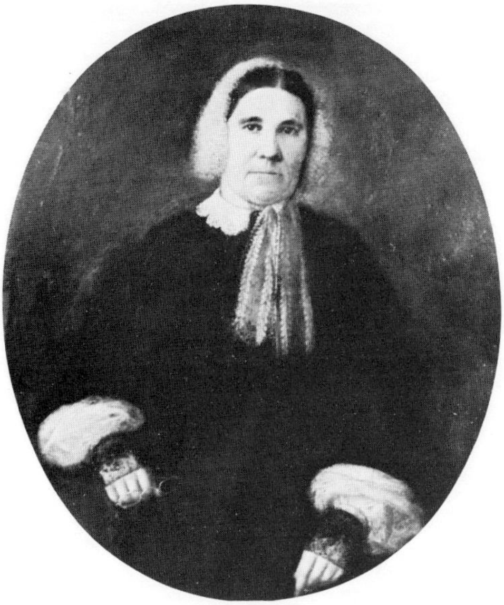

BERNARD, FRANCISCO
Portrait of woman
(signed "F. Bernard, 1859")
42" x 32"

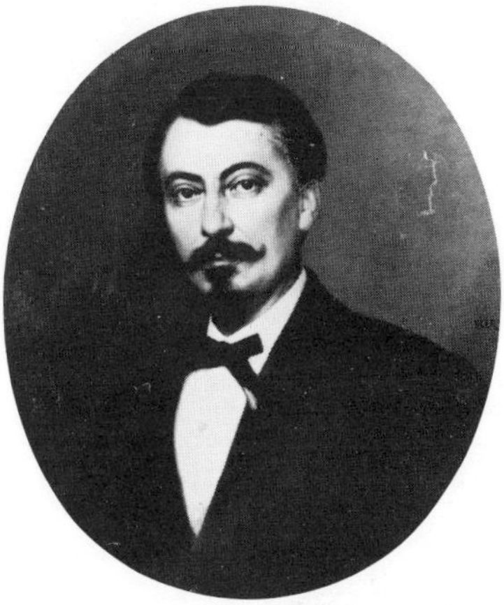

BERNARD, FRANCISCO
Portrait of man
(signed, "Bernard, 1870")
30" x 25"

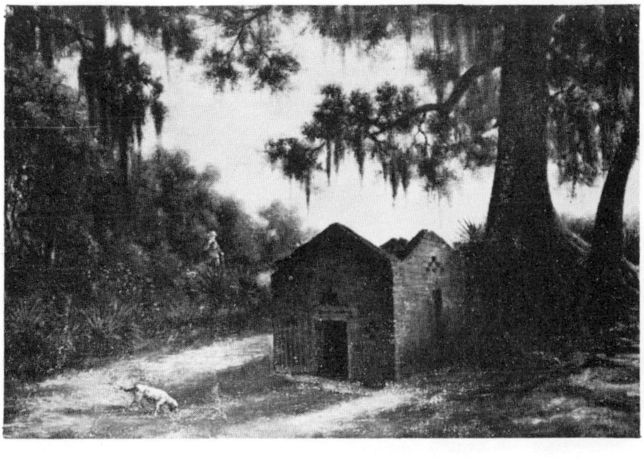

BERNARD, FRANCISCO
Hunter and dog near a ruined building
(signed) 14" x 20"

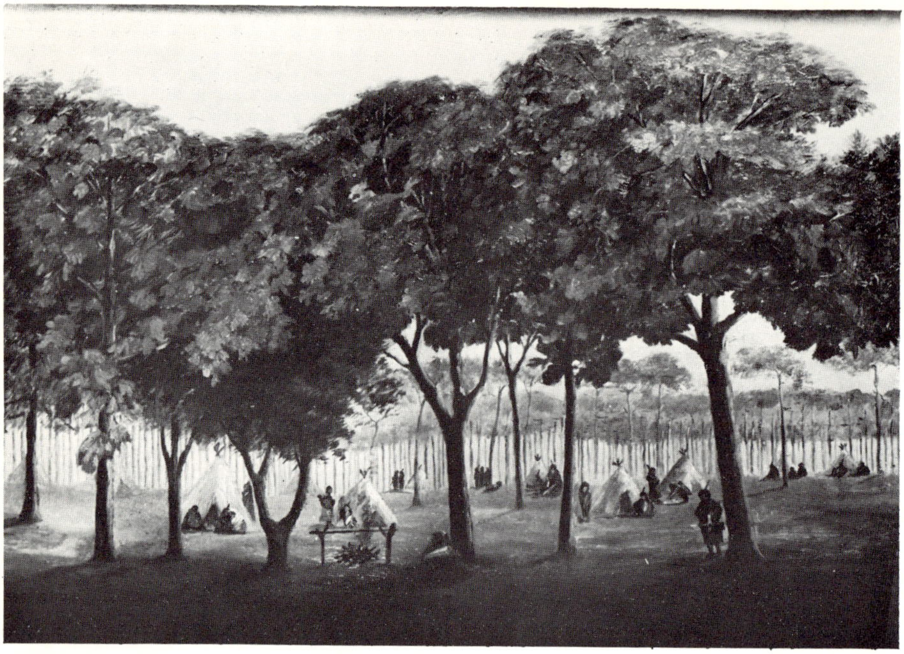

BERNARD, FRANCISCO (signed)
Indian Encampment
17¾" x 23¾"

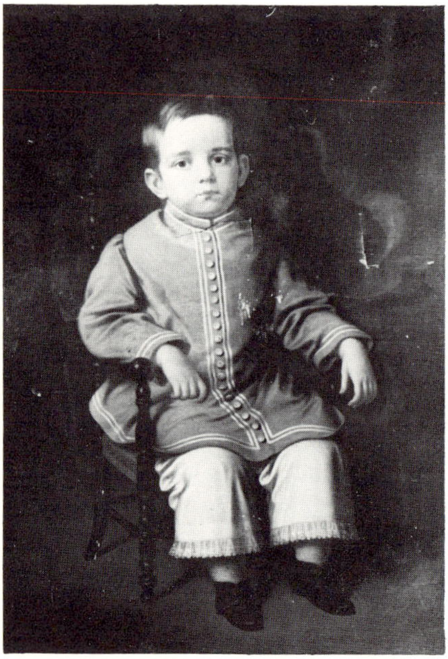

BERNARD, FRANCISCO (attrib.)
Boy of the Beauregard family, painted in the 1850s.
39½" x 31½"

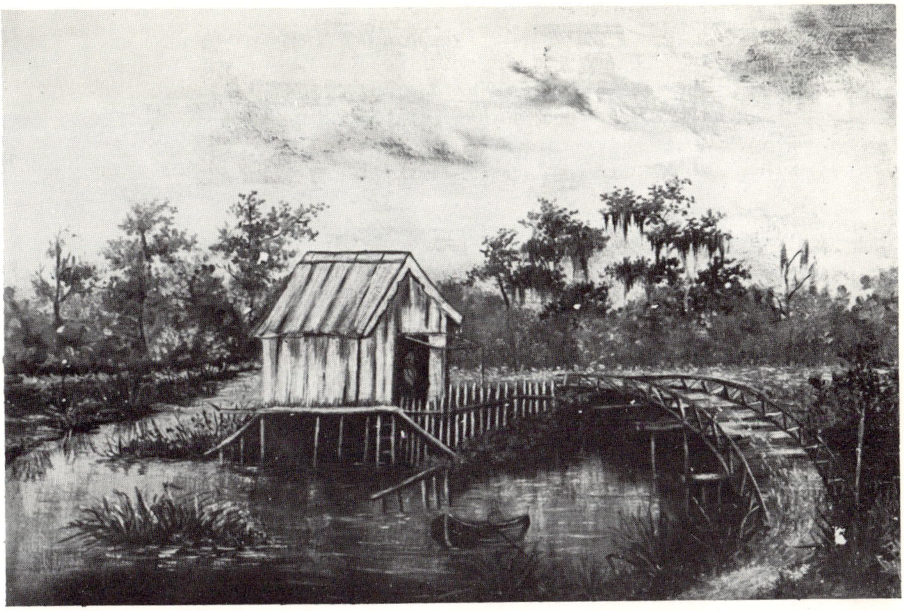

(signed, 1870)

BLAMERS, B.
Bridge over a bayou
10" x 14"

Blamers, B.

The local scene is revealed in paintings by the untrained as well as by the professional. Blamers is known only by a signature on this view of a charming spot on a Louisiana bayou.

The Louisiana Bayou Landscape resembles neither that of the Asiatic tropics nor the middle American; it is an intermingling of temperate and subtropical vegetation. Architecturally speaking, the palm thatch roof is absent. The dwelling sits on poles for two reasons, sanitation and flood protection. Hurricane winds, too, will often drive under and over the house on stilts and leave it standing.

It is warm and humid and lazy — fish and shallfish abound, and with some corn and sweet potatoes, life can be sustained amicably. Of course there are snakes and insect, but when were we without them.

Blanchard, Blanche Virginia, 1866-1959

Born in New Orleans, trained in music, drama and the arts, in Emmetsburg, Md. at the Academy of the Daughters of Charity. Later moved to Washington, D. C., where she studied under Andrews at the Corcoran Gallery in 1888. She copied paintings in the Corcoran, as was the custom, and was befriended by President Grover Cleveland, of whom she painted a portrait for the White House.

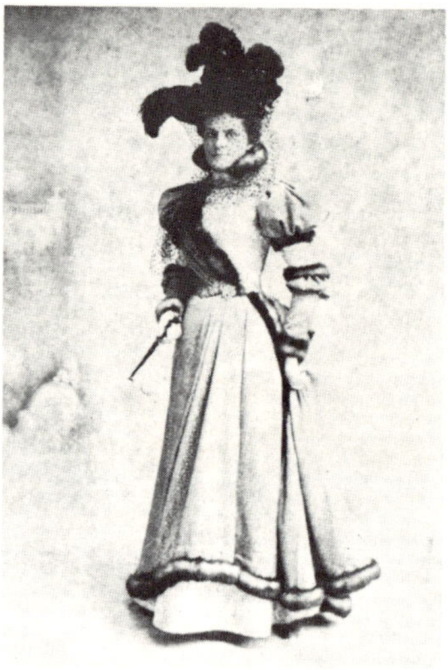

Photograph of Blanche Blanchard

After her return to New Orleans, she painted extensively portraits and landscapes, and studied with C. Giroux (viz.). Here she developed a fine landscape style, particularly in her orange-skyed atmospheric Louisiana tidewater scenes. Her cabin scenes are fine depictations and can be classed with Walker, Rudolph, Andrieu and Molinary. There is a mother of pearl atmosphere over her landscapes, and an alligator lying on a bayou bank is a recognizable mannerism. The paintings are signed generally with a small red B.B. or the full script signature as on the Behan portrait (viz.).

In 1893 we have a record of her being listed in the *Charter Constitution and By Laws of the Artists Assn. of N.O., 1893, Hopkins Prtg. Co., 22 Commercial Place, N.O.* She married the Architect, Charles Milo Williams, of New Orleans, was an accomplished harpist, and with her husband made their residence at 1035 Carrollton a focal point for art and music in the city.

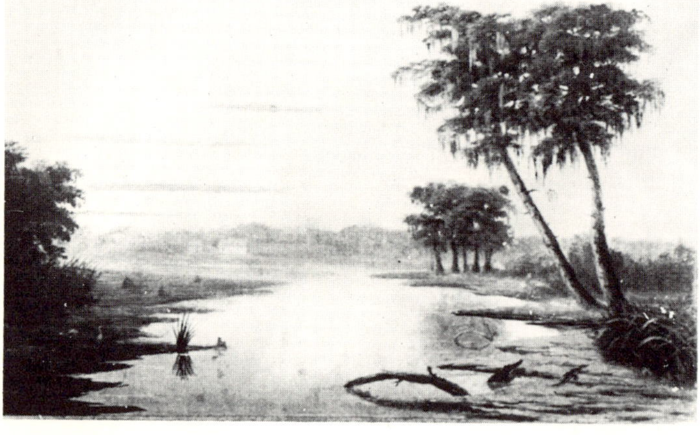

BLANCHE BLANCHARD
Swamp Scene 10" x 14"

(signed, B.B.)

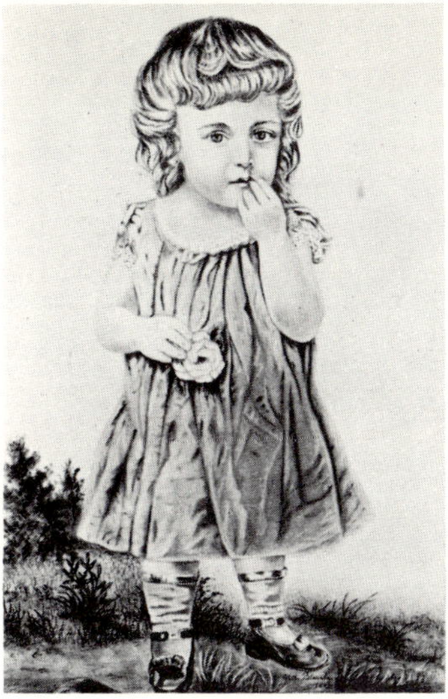

Drawing by STELLA BLANCHARD
Sister of Blanche, a gifted amateur
27½" x 14¼"

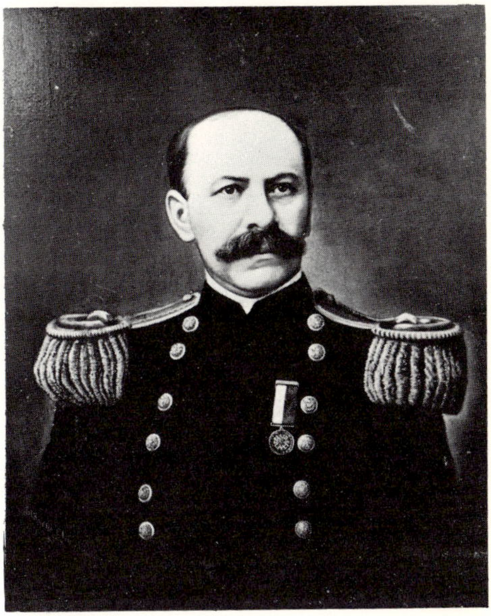

BLANCHE BLANCHARD (signed '93)
Portrait believed to be Major Wm. J. Behan
30" x 25"

Major Behan was Mayor of New Orleans (1882), a Major in the Washington Artillery, and Colonel of the Louisiana Field Artillery in charge at the capture of the State Government of La. by the Citizens' Soldiery, 1874. (ref. Washington Artillery Annual, 1894 in the Jackson Barracks Library, N.O.)

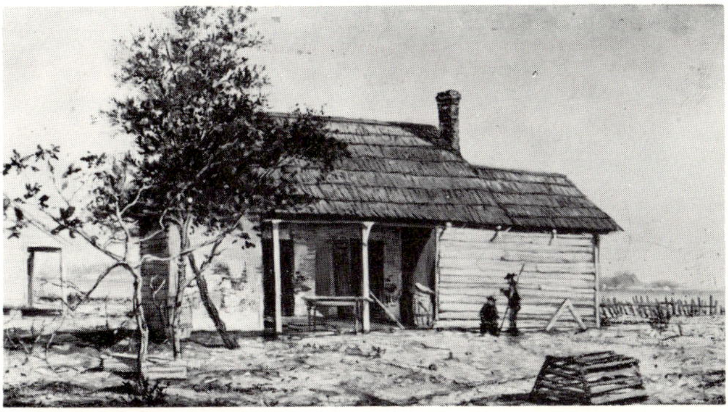

BLANCHE BLANCHARD (signed B.B.)
Cabin 6¼" x 11"

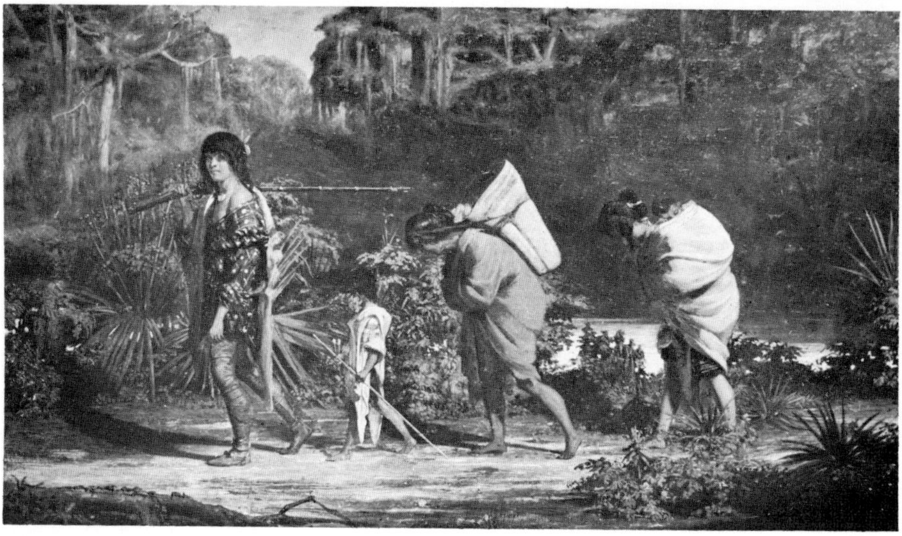

BOISSEAU, ALFRED (signed "Al. Boisseau")
"Marche d'Indiens de la Louisiane"
Choctaws in Louisiana 20" x 40"
Courtesy Isaac Delgado Mus. of Art, N.O.
Gift of W. E. Groves

Boisseau, Alfred 1823-1901

Born in Paris, studied with Paul Delaroche, exhibited at the Salon in 1842, painted portraits that have a slight primitive quality, and some genre. He did, however, in the writer's opinion paint the most informative painting of Southeastern Indians, the much depicted "Marche d'Indiens de la Louisiane." Painted in the 1840's, this was one of the transitory groups of the five civilized tribes, which during their removal to Oklahoma passed through Louisiana. It is virtually the only costume record contemporary with Catlin and Charles Bird King, and is a magnificent document; from the silver studded flintlock and shell ornamented dress of the father to the blowgun and darts of the son and the tumpline-carrying, ornamented basket of wife 1 and the maternal quality of wife 2. The vestigial Seminole-Choctaw stripe, which is still seen on the Florida Seminoles, shows clearly near the knee of the younger woman. All this takes place in a palmetto studded watery landscape, which has never been surpassed in Louisiana painting.

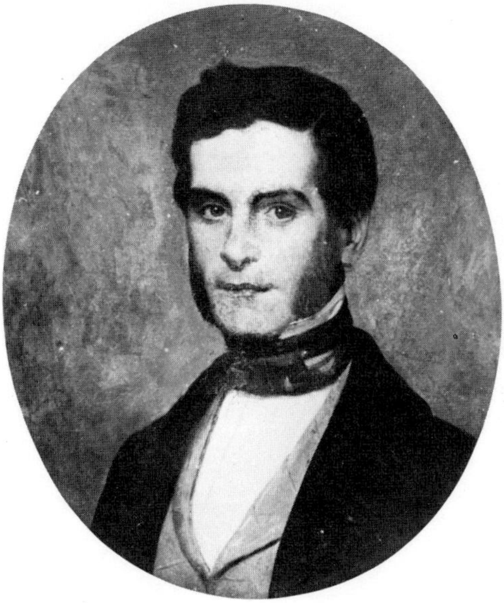

BOISSEAU, ALFRED
Portrait of Man
signed 1848
23" x 20"

Boisseau was in New Orleans in 1845-46, and exhibited in New York in 1849 and 52. A portrait and landscape painter of his name, advertising as a teacher and dealer in Art, in Cleveland, Ohio in 1852, may be this same Boisseau, but paintings by him exist in Louisiana as late as 1859.

About 1860 he settled in Montreal, where he painted many portraits of Montreal Society. He died in Buffalo, New York.

Boyle, Charles Wellington, 1860-1925

Born in New Orleans, Father J. F. Boyle, lived at Lewisburg, La. Mother Bertha F. Fortich. Studied at the New York School of Art; The Art Students League; and with Poincy and Molinary in New Orleans. Taught in the Art Assn. School of Arts, New Orleans; at Ruston College, Ruston, La.; at Home Institute, and Valence Institute, and Ferrels School for Boys in New Orleans.

He was the second director of the Delgado Museum from 1922 until his death.

He can be truly classed as one of the early La. impressionists and his "Cypress Studded Coastline" is near his estate in Mandeville. The Mandeville house was a gathering place for the fin de siecle artists of Louisiana, including the Ellsworths, Pemberton, Mayfield, Molinary, Westfeld.

There are nine paintings in the W. E. Groves collection, of which three of the Louisiana subjects are reproduced here.

BOYLE, C. W.
Lakeshore near Mandeville
10" x 17"

(signed)

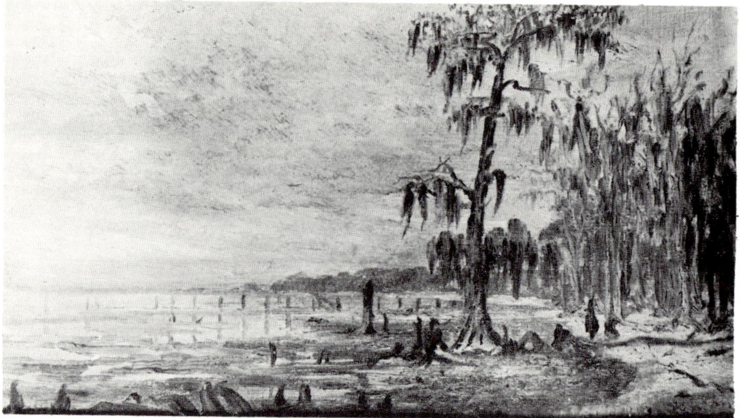

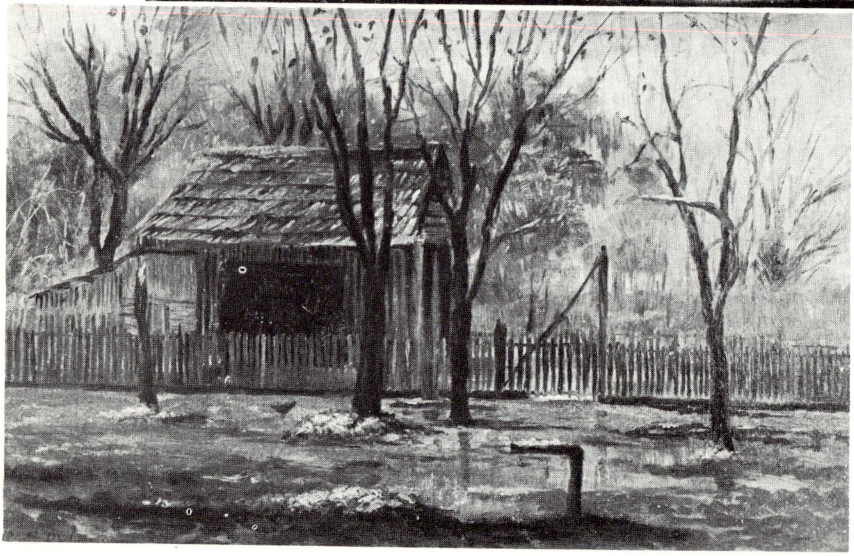

BOYLE, C. W. Louisiana Winter 11¼" x 17½" (signed)

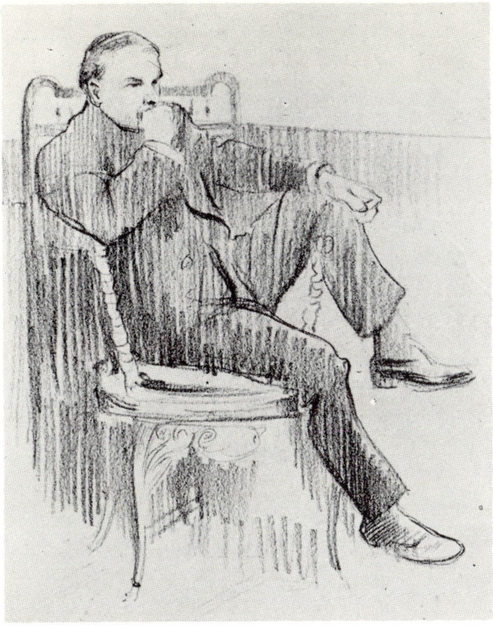

Pencil Portrait of Boyle,
drawn by Mayfield at the
"Sketch Club"

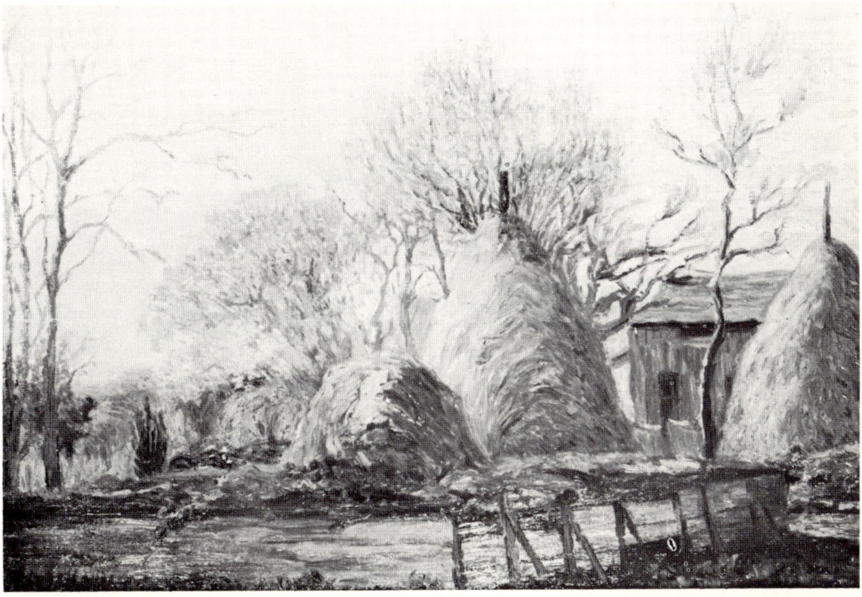

(signed)

BOYLE, C. W.
Haystacks
18" x 25½"

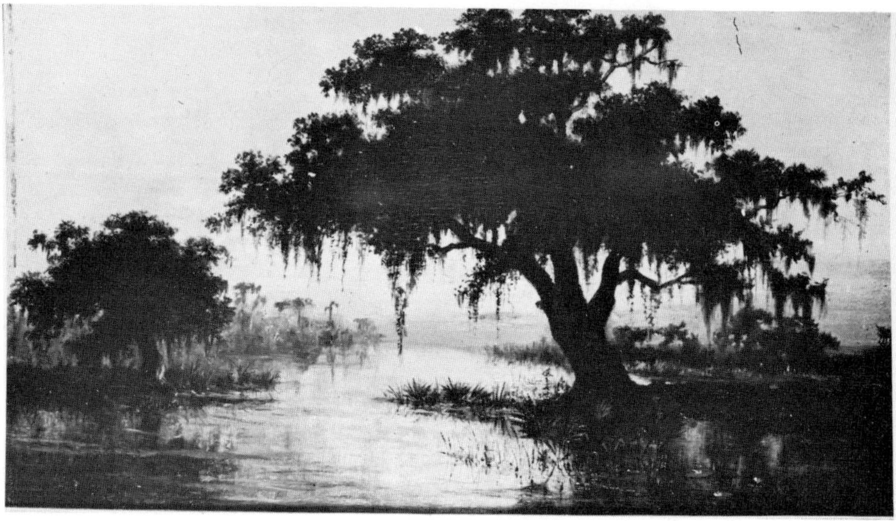

BUCK, WM. H. (signed)
Live Oak on Water's Edge
12" x 20"

Buck, William H., 1840-1888

Born in Norway, migrated to Boston, thence to New Orleans. While working for a cotton broker, studied with Clague (viz.) and Ciceri, first exhibiting in 1877. In 1880 he set himself up as a full time artist with a studio at 26 Carondelet St. In the short years of his painting career he turned out an amazing number of landscapes, the best of them very much in the manner of his teacher Richard Clague. Some of his pot boilers show evidence of borrowing subject matter from the engravings in current publications such as "Picturesque America", but he put his own individual stamp on them, and Buck, along with Clague, Rudolph, Marshall Smith, Giroux, Blanchard and Walker, is inextricably linked with the world of plantations, bayous and moss-hung bird-haunted swamps.

His paintings exhibit three distinct styles, first the blue-white style where the landscape is sunny and illuminated, reflecting the sound workmanship of Richard Clague; the second, brown and involuted, of deep philosophical bend, in Poe's words "the ghoul-haunted woodland of weir", where rapacious and insatiable cormorants and vultures contemplate lone travelers from swamp tree tops; and finally his paintings become enveloped in the brown soup style which afflicted so many late 19th century painters, whose creations drown in unstable pigments.

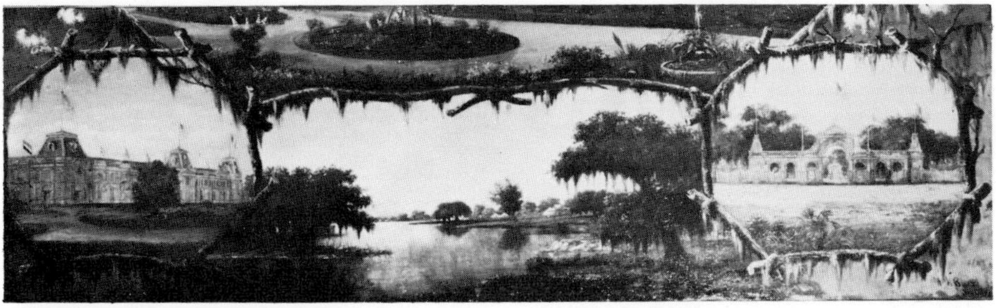

BUCK, WM. H.
The Cotton Exposition, N. O., 21" x 72"

signed "W. H. Buck, New Orleans"

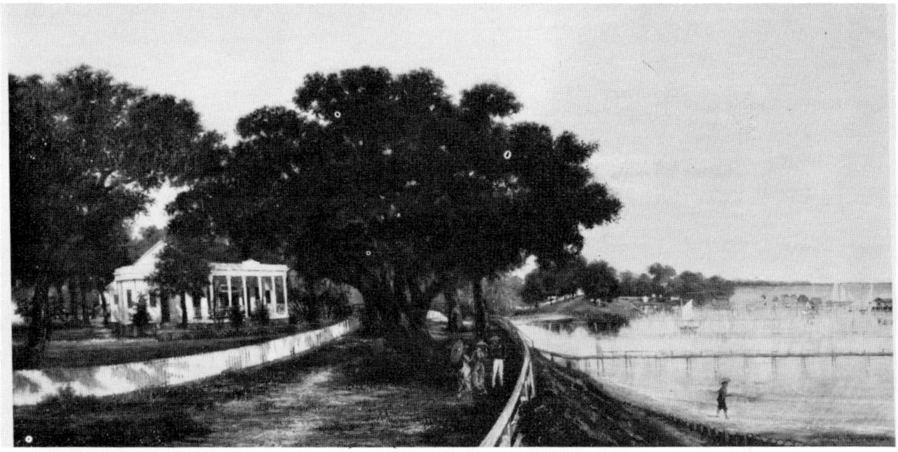

BUCK, WM. H.
Gulf Coast Scene, 18" x 25"
Courtesy A. Hayes Town

Signed "Wm. H. Buck"

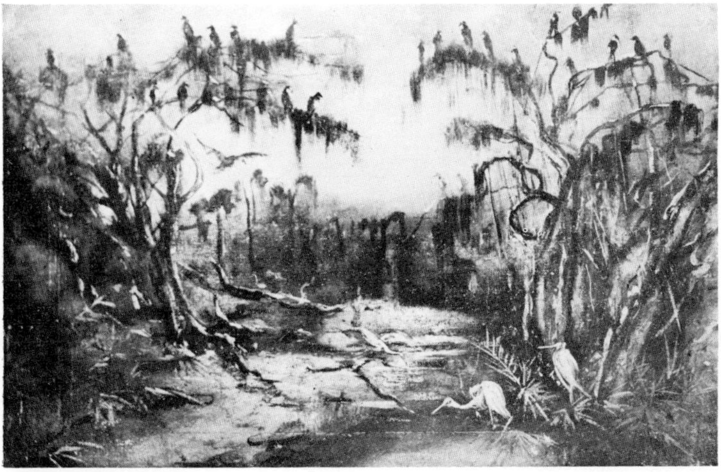

BUCK, WM. H.
Landscape with Vultures, 12" x 16"

Signed "Wm. H. Buck"

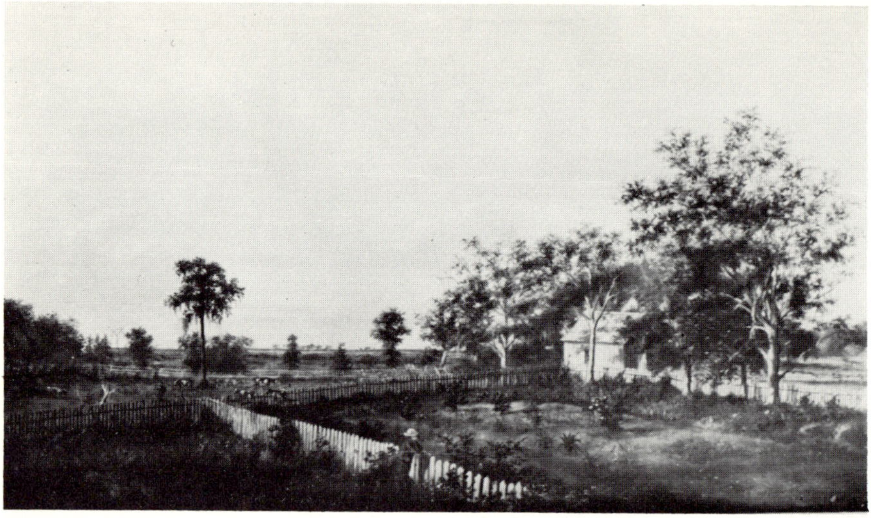

BUCK, WH. H.
Louisiana Farm
12" x 20"

signed

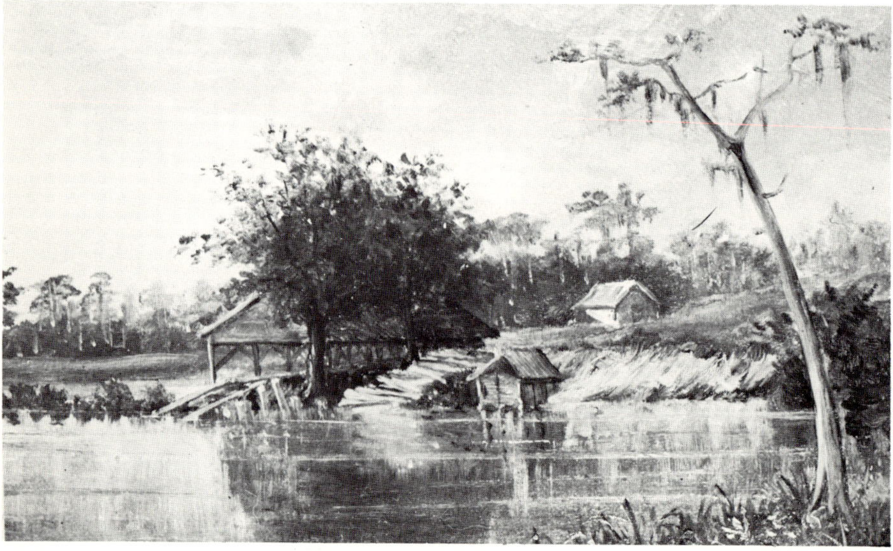

BUCK, WM. H.
Boat House
8" x 12"

signed "Sketch by Buck"

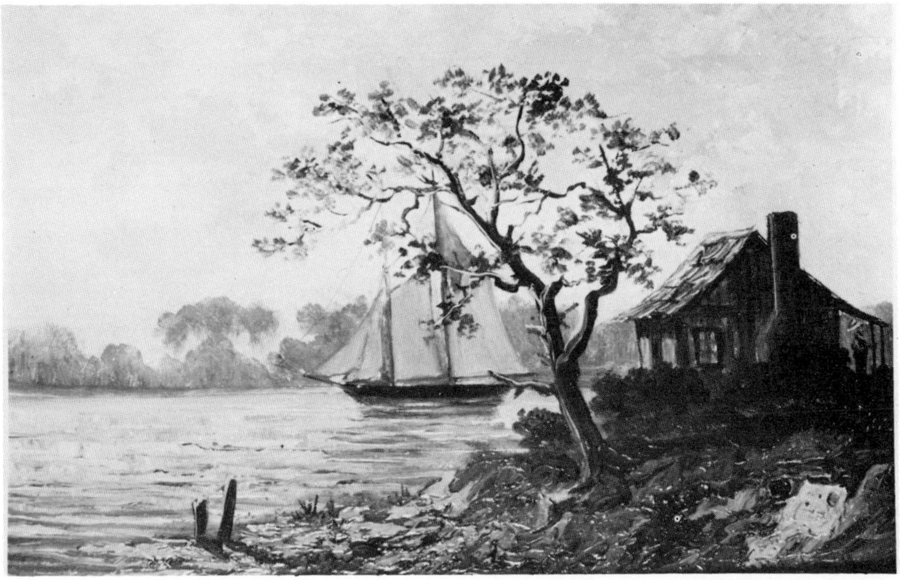

BUCK, WM. H.
Cabin and Sailboat
8" x 12"

Signed "Sketch by Buck"

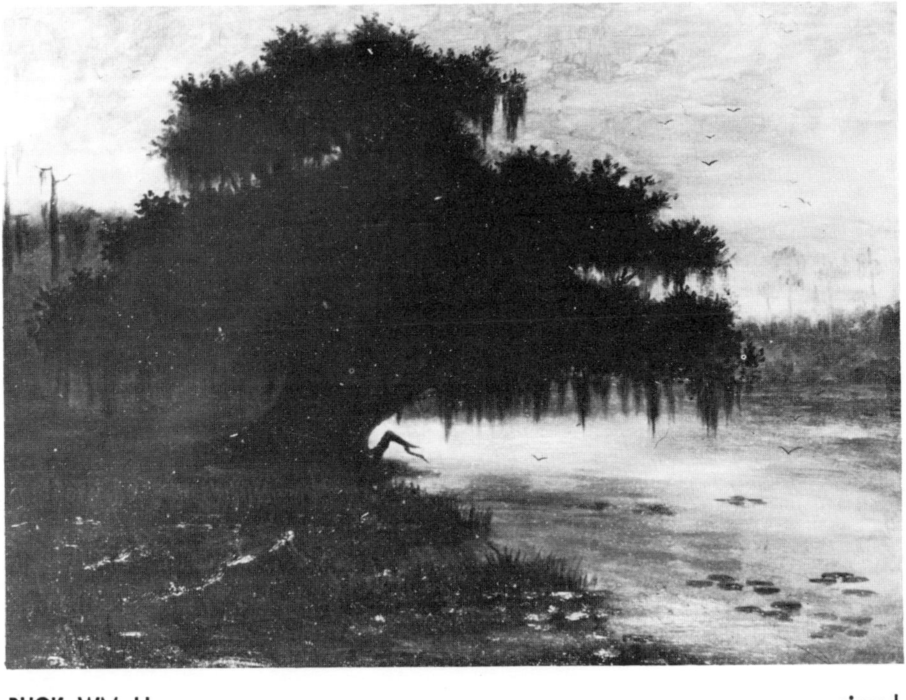

BUCK, WM. H.
Live Oak
20½" x 24½"

signed

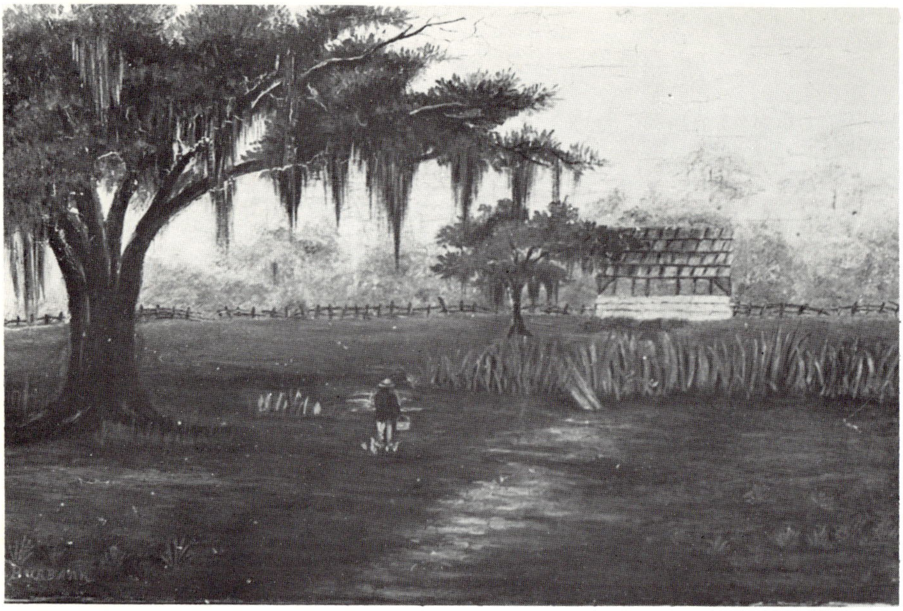

BURBANK, S. signed
The Egg-hunter
11" x 16"

Two amateur painters recording the Louisiana rural scene.

Rural Louisiana farm operations were seldom painted. The cotton field had its Walker, the architecture its Clague and Smith, the river its Norieri, but it was left to Burbank to immortalize the visit to the chicken house — a lovely and homely walk with the egg basket.

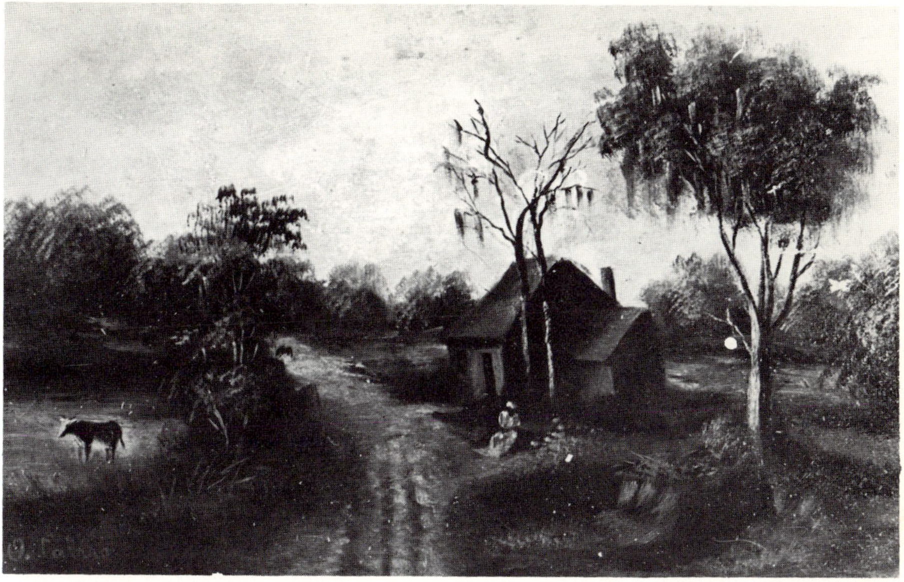

CABIRO, O. signed
The Gourd Tree

In Audubon's *Birds of America*, there is the print of the purple martin nesting in a gourd. It was common practice to hang these gourds, with a martin-sized entrance hole, in a tree. The martins kept the house area virtually free of insects, a sort of ornithological fogging.

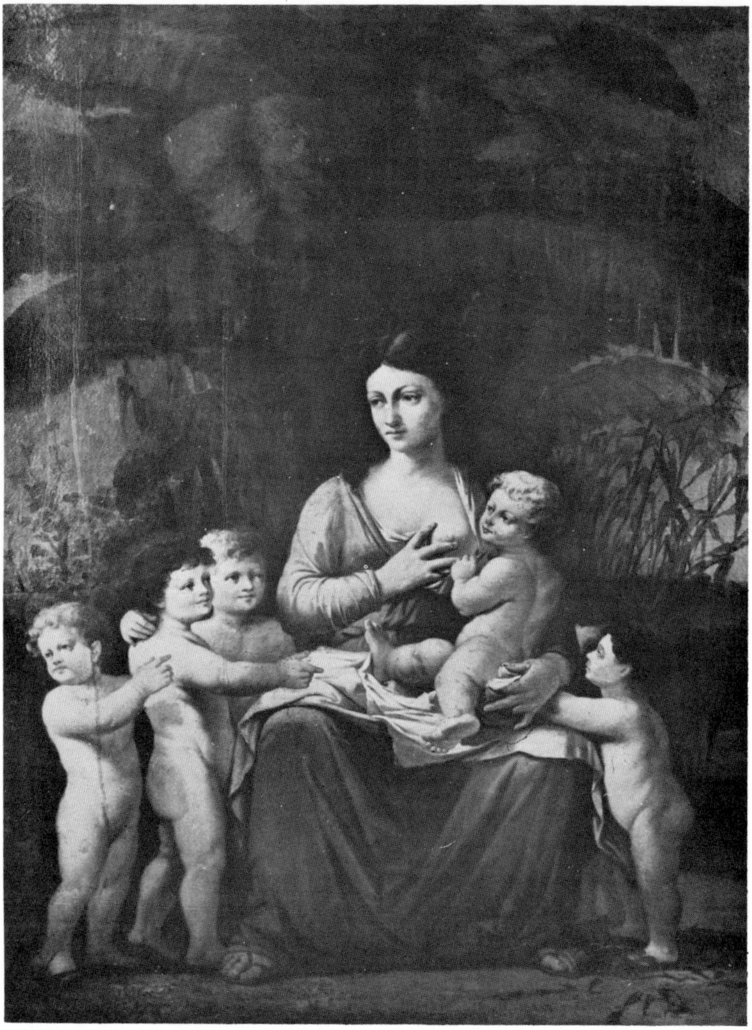

CANOVA, DOMINICO
Mother Louisiana (showing cane and cotton in background)
45" x 27"

Canova, Dominico, 1800? - ca. 1869

Working for the lithographer Anthony Imbert in New York City in 1825; thought to be the D. Canova who appears first in the New Orleans City Directory in 1840, referred to as "returning" to that city, after three years of teaching at Jefferson College; active for the next three decades in New Orleans as a painter and teacher. He is reputed to have been a mural and decorative painter as his easel paintings attest. Some wall paintings survive in a private residence, which are almost certainly by his hand and he decorated the walls of the St. Louis Exchange (Coulon's notes).

In 1861 he was doing scene painting at the opera house, and was living on St. Bernard on the "raquette plains". Before that he is listed at 80 Royal, 1840-41, St. Philip and Marais, 1842, then as artist and painter, 6 Annette, 1851 and 1853, and at 243 Canal St in 1854.

We know nothing of his birth, but his style points to Italy. Tradition says that he is the Nephew of Antonio Canova, the well known sculptor.

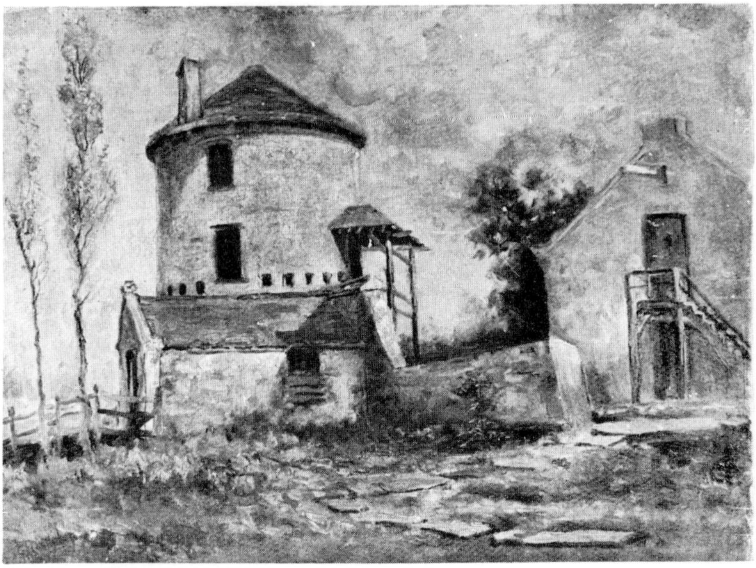

CASTLEDEN, GEORGE F. signed
Jackson Barracks
14" x 18"

Castleden, George F., 1861- ?

Born in Canterbury, Kent, England, studied under Sir Thomas Sidney Cooper. Won prizes at Canterbury, and in Canada at Regina, Winnipeg, and Toronto. (ref. I. M. Cline; Contemporary Art and Artists in New Orleans, 1924). Came to New Orleans sometime after the turn of the century, did interior decorating and theatrical scenery and oil and watercolor landscapes. The pictured example of his work is the historic Jackson Barracks, erected in 1834. Anthony Drain gets credit for finding the site, Lt. F. W. Wilkinson drew the plans in ca. 1830, and a Capt. Clark supervised the construction. First called New Orleans Barracks, in 1848 changed to United States Barracks. A Martello tower is clearly visible in the painting. This was a heavily fortified artillery platform, which was used in repelling warships. Another Martello tower is in the Bayou Dupre in Lake Borgne.

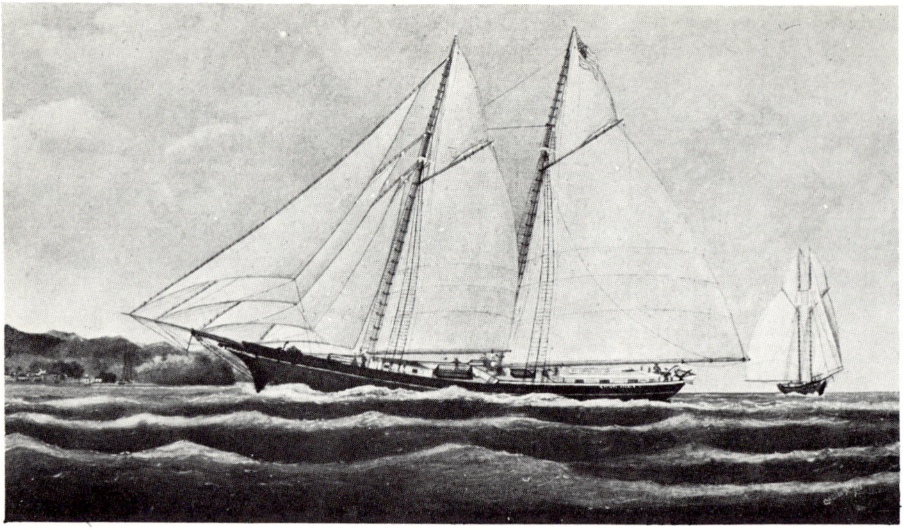

CHALLONER, WM. L.
Two Schooners
14" x 24"

signed, "Challoner/'85"

Challoner, William L. (late 19th century)

Very little is known about Challoner, although a good many of his paintings exist. He painted many in the New Orleans harbor, and also on the west coast. It is thought in Oregon that he was a ship captain. His exact detail in the recording of both ships and shoreline is romanticized by his treatment of sky, waves and bird life. He observed, too, the air pollution caused by the increasing number of steamboats in the rivers and harbors, with their billowing black smoke.

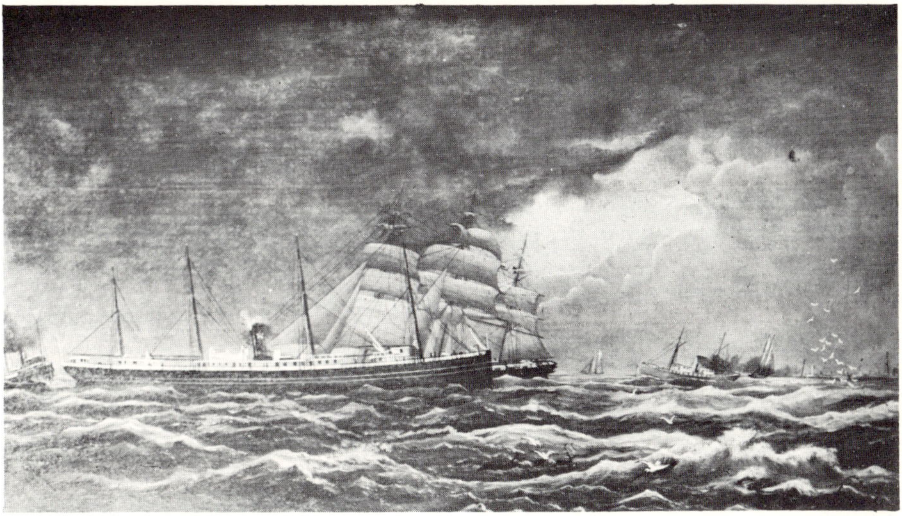

CHALLONER, WM. L. signed
Morgan Liner and Square Rigger
14" x 24"

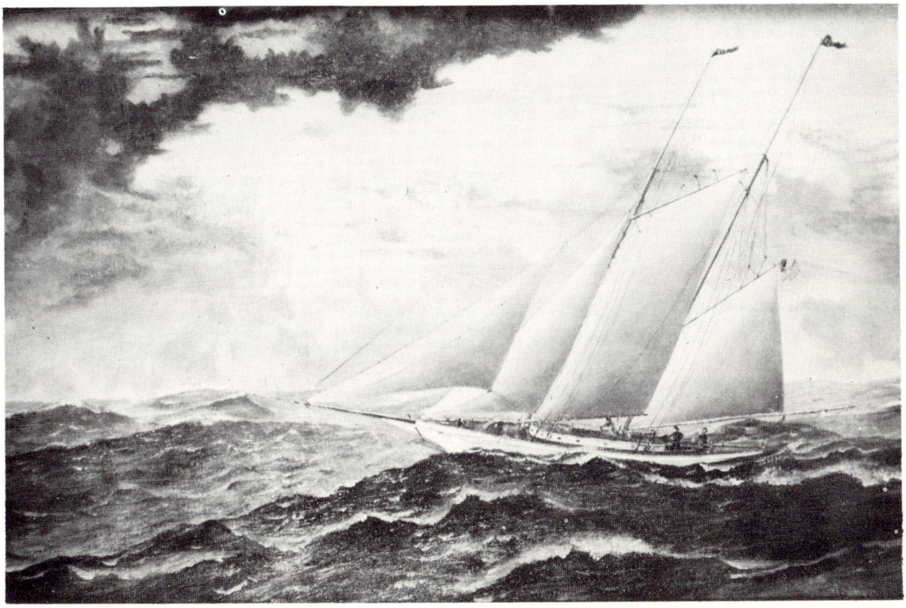

CHALLONER, WM. L. signed
Rough Waters
15" x 23"

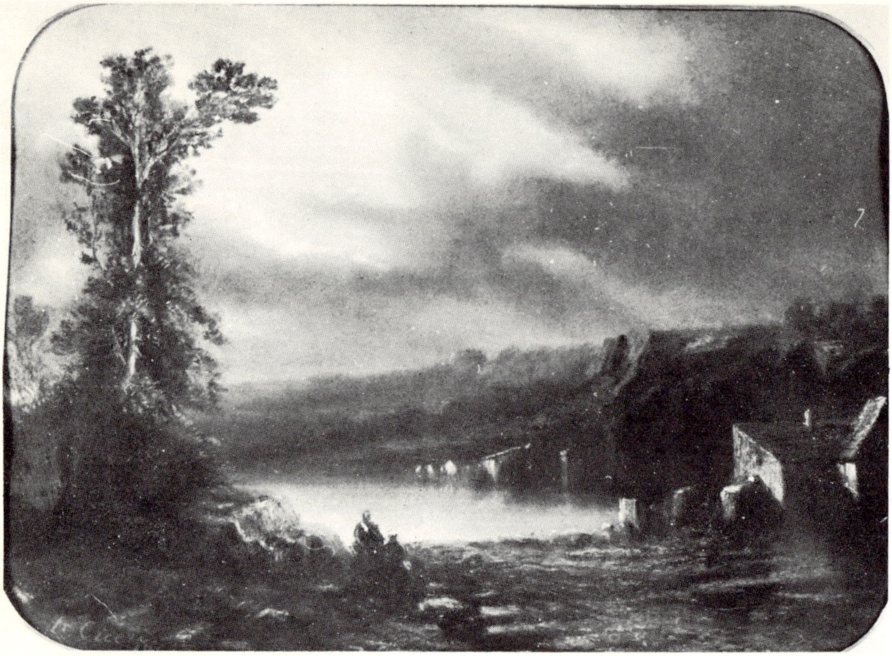

CICERI, ERNEST
Moonlit Landscape
Pastel, 10" x 13½"

signed

Ciceri, Ernest, 1817-1866

Came to New Orleans in 1859 to paint conjointly with Devalle the scenery of the French Opera House. He was the son of P. L. C. Ciceri, a painter well known in France, and the grandson of Eugene Isabey, a famous miniature painter.

In New Orleans, Ciceri's admirers classed him as "the father of modern scenic painting". He was a teacher of painting, but insisted he knew nothing of drawing. He had, however, a high opinion of the quality of his work. When he sold one of his charming watercolors or pastels his usual comment was, "I have given you gold for lead". (ref. article by Marcia Davies in "Men and Matters" preserved in Dr. Cline's scrapbook, W. E. Groves archives.)

Clague, Richard, Jr., 1821-1873

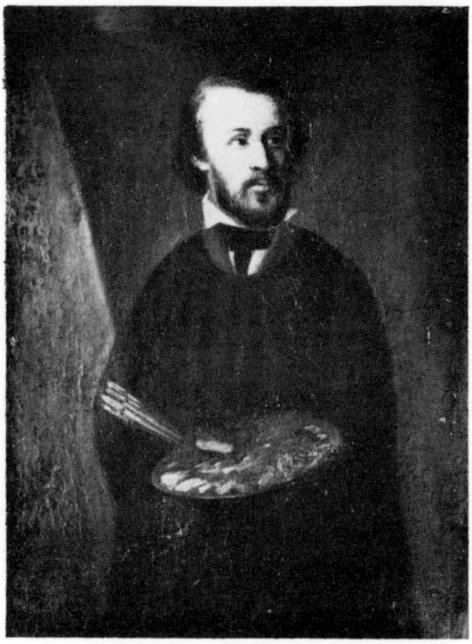

CLAGUE, R., Self-portrait

19" x 13"

Native of Louisiana, son of a Manxman who came to America and married Justine de la Roche of New Orleans. Richard Clague Sr.'s fortune made in shipping, banking, insurance and the slave trade, left his son financially independent; Richard Jr. had already been at school at St. Humbert's Academy in Switzerland, when he decided to go back to France and attend the Ecole des Beaux Arts, Paris. Studied with Ernest Hebert there and later with Leon Pomarede the Mississippi Panorama painter in New Orleans.

In the 1850s he enrolled in a French expedition as draughtsman to explore for the source of the Nile, under Egyptian sponsorship. A sketchbook owned by the Delgado Museum, contains pencil drawings of this expedition, as well as some sketches for his future Louisiana paintings. In 1861 he served as an officer in the New Orleans Blues under Bernard de Marigny. The war depleted his estate and he actively went into painting. The great series of Louisiana paintings emanate from this period. His relatively rare portraits, as in the case of his three self portraits (one in the Louisiana State Museum, one in private hands, and one in the Groves collection) plus the portraits of his wife and children, also in private hands, are the epitome of portrait painting in Louisiana, and in the writer's opinion are the logical culmination of the Feuille, Amans and Vaudechamps styles.

He advertised in 1851 in New Orleans as an artist, and is listed in the directories for 1854-55 without occupation.

According to G. D. Coulon's notes, Clague studied with Pomarede—c. 1842-43 and in Paris "entered the studio of Ingres" (not substantiated elsewhere); later " was sent as draughtsman by the Pasha of Egypt with a party of French Savants, to discover the source of the Nile. There were 40, only 11 came back. They buried the others along the road. After this unsuccessful attempt he came back to New Orleans and opened a studio with P. Poincy on Camp St. and painted some good portraits and many Louisiana views."

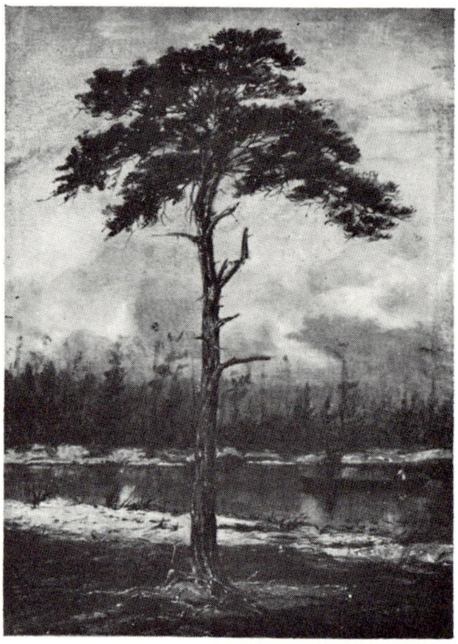

CLAGUE, RICHARD
Pine in Bayou, 14" x 10"
not signed, identified from Clague's sketchbook in the Isaac Delgado Museum, N.O.

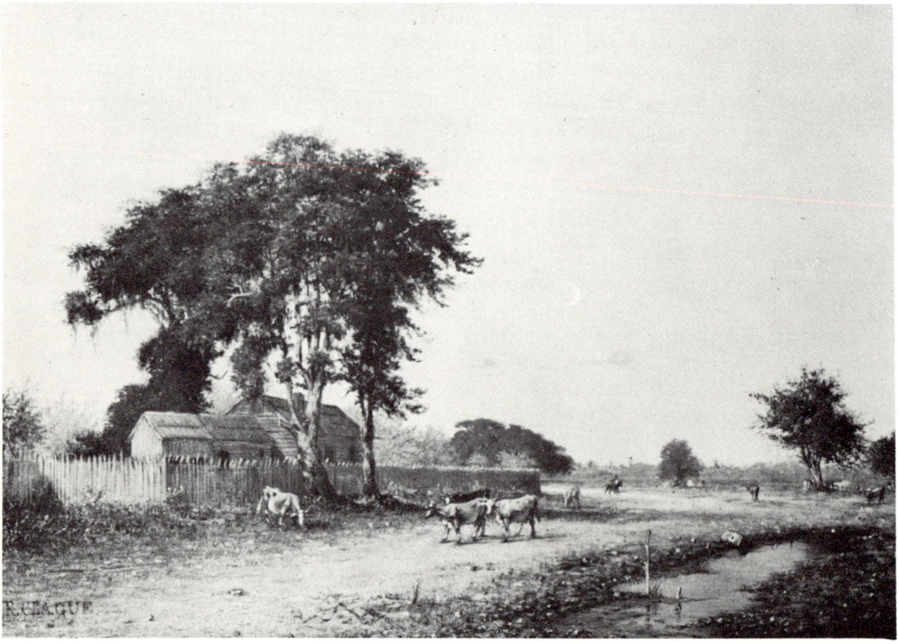

CLAGUE, RICHARD
Rural Scene, Louisiana

signed, "R. Clague"

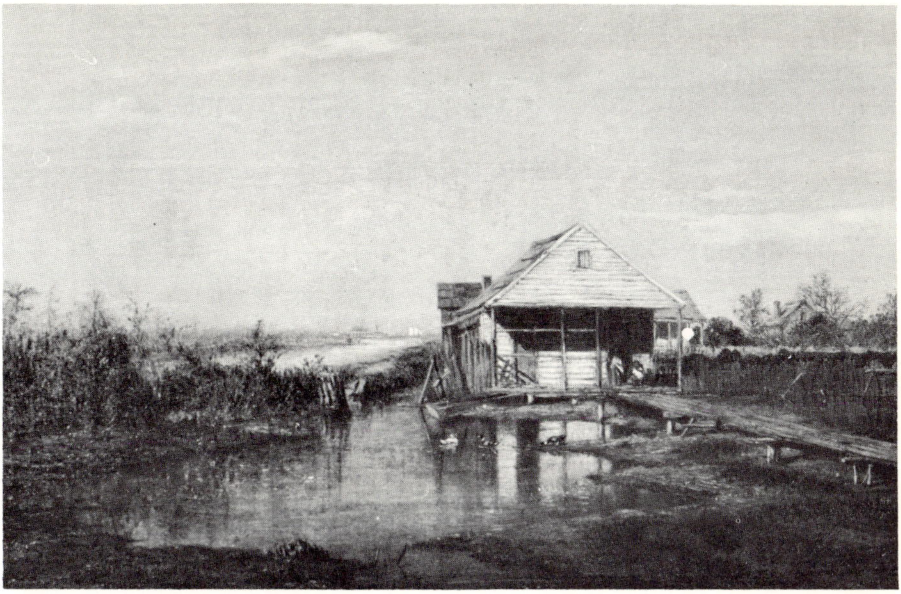

Courtesy Hays Town, Baton Rouge

These two very similar paintings of a "Trapper's Cabin" by Clague were both originally in the W. E. Groves Collection.

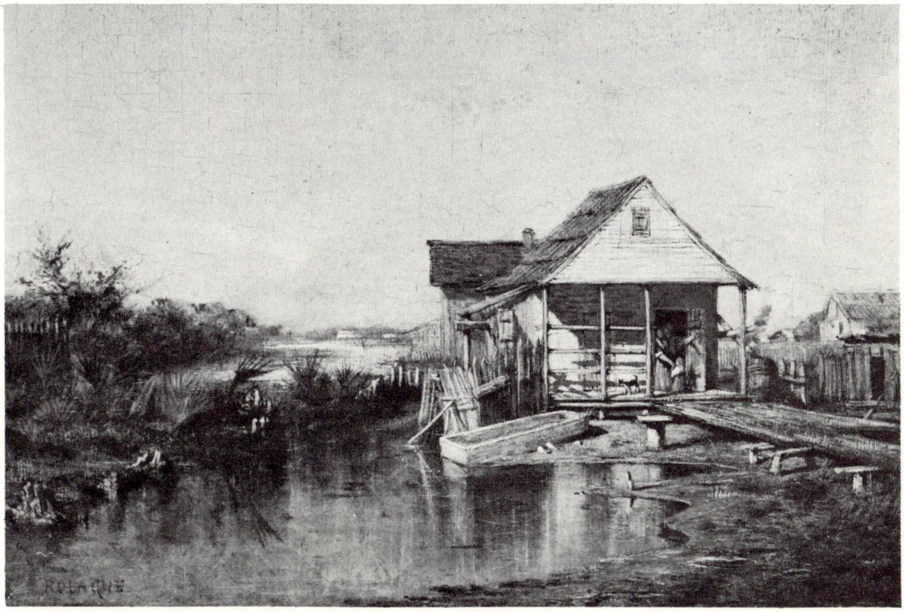

Courtesy Isaac Delgado Museum, New Orleans, 12" x 16" (signed)
Gift of W. E. Groves

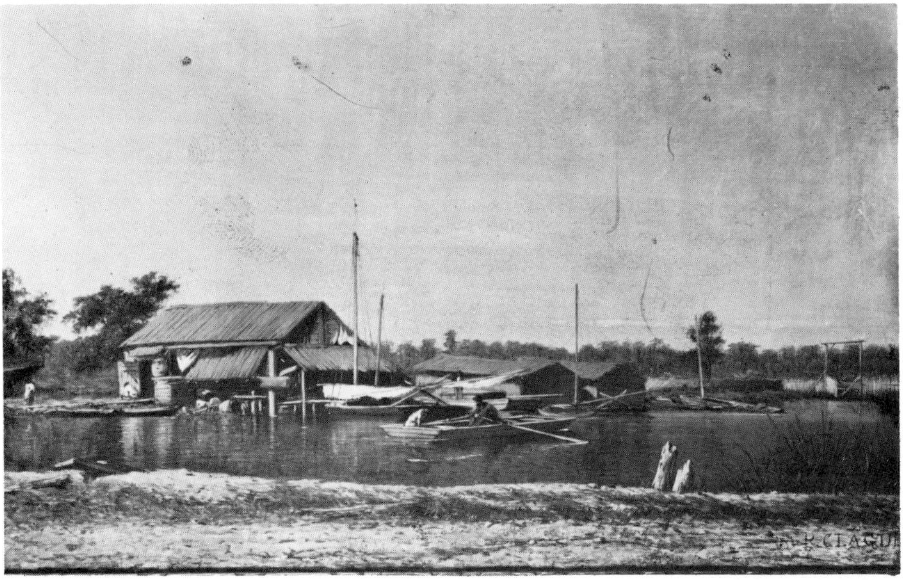

CLAGUE, RICHARD
Bayou Scene
16" x 24½"

Signed "R. Clague"

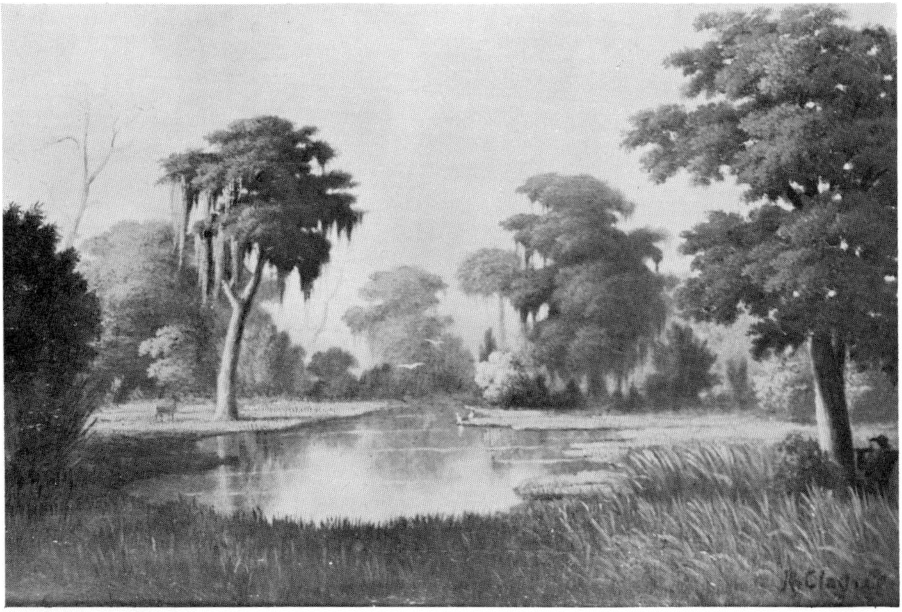

CLAGUE, RICHARD
The Deer Hunter
12" x 18"

Signed "R. Clague"

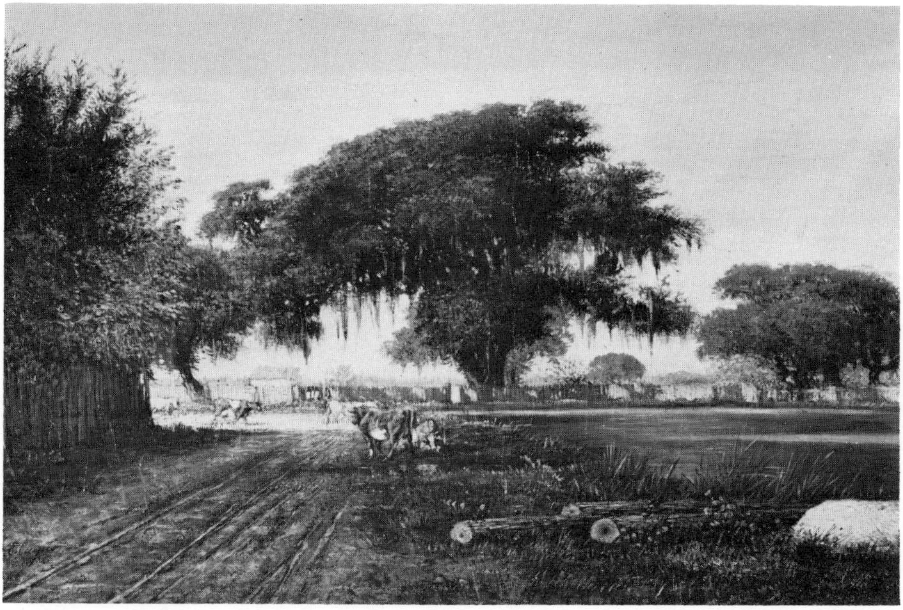

CLAGUE, RICHARD
Landscape (probably in Tammany Parish)
oil on canvas, 15" x 24½"
Courtesy Anglo-American Mus., Baton Rouge, La.
Gift of W. E. Groves

Signed in script "R. Clague"

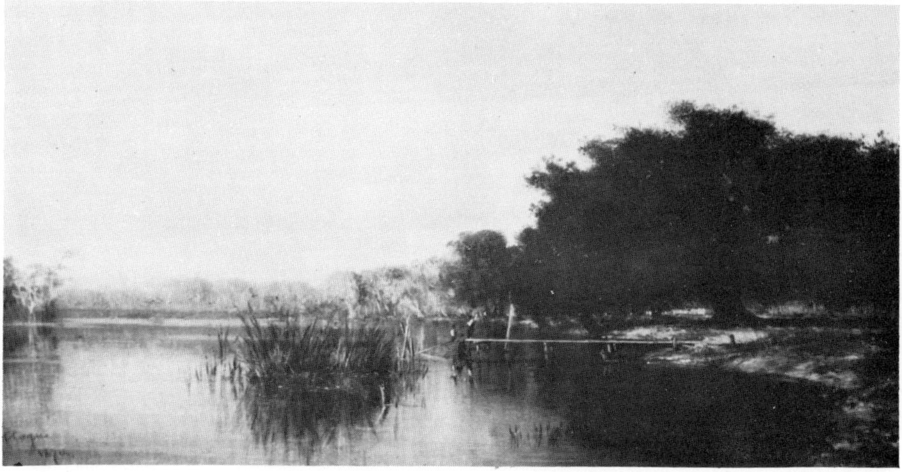

CLAGUE, RICHARD
Bayou Fishing Camp, 17" x 30"

signed, 1870

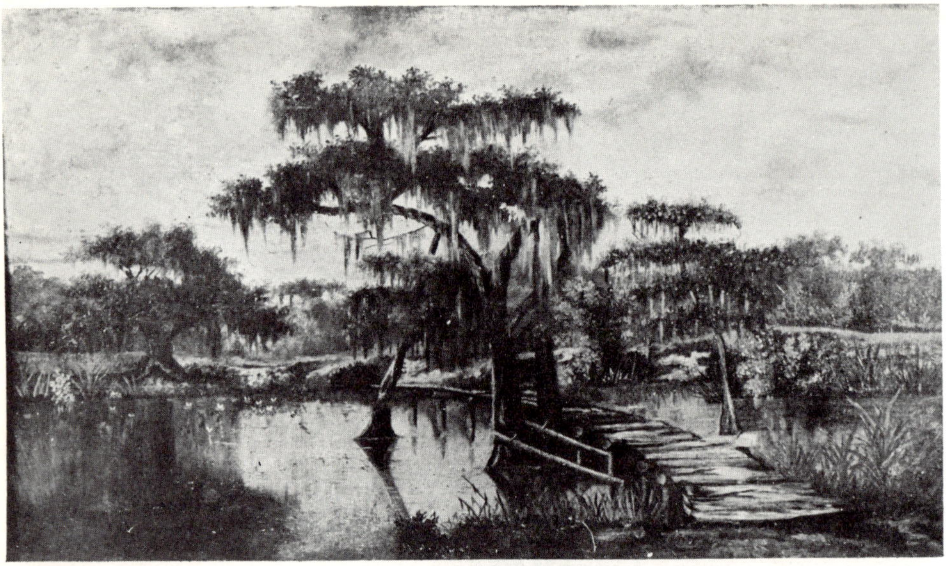

COOPER, E. S. signed
Bayou, 18" x 30"

Cooper, E. S. (dates unknown)

Said by Dr. Cline to be an Englishman who painted for a time in the New Orleans area.

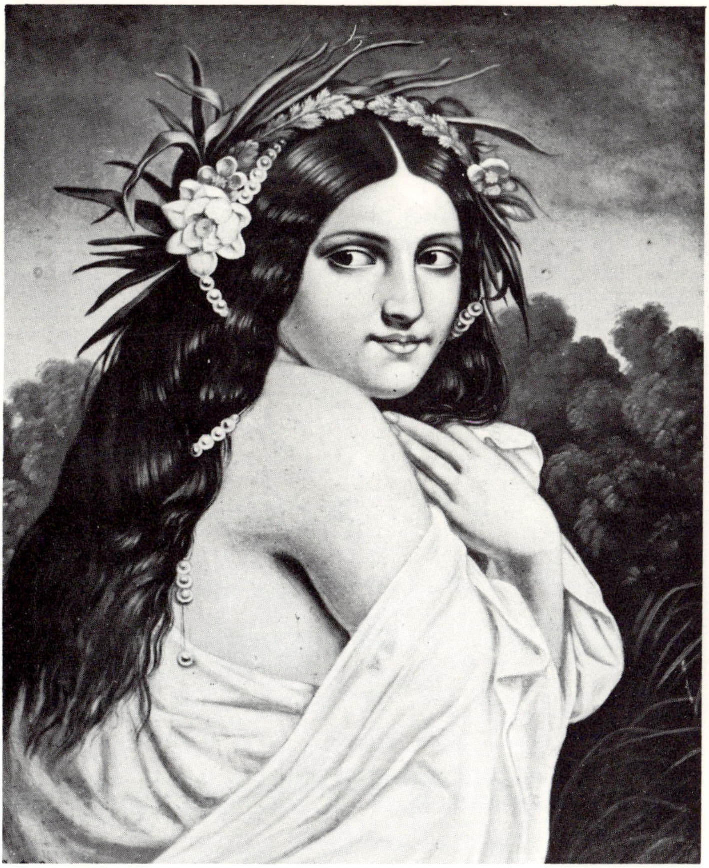

COULON, G. D.
Spirit of Louisiana
45" x 27"

signed G.D.C. '94

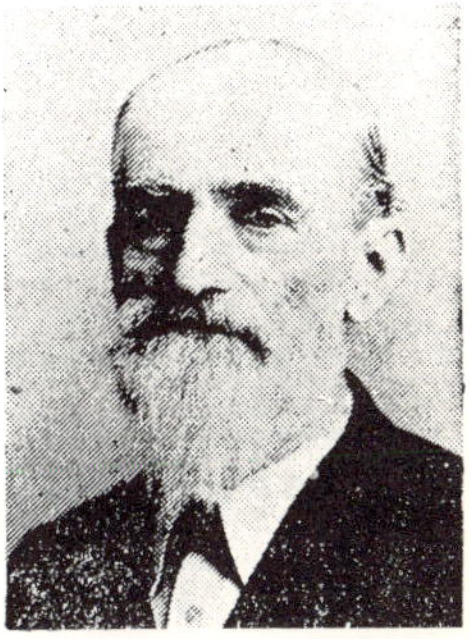

Coulon, George D., 1822-1904

Born in Selancourt (Doubs), France, came to New Orleans at age 11. Learned drawing at public school under Toussaint Bigot, formerly teacher at the College of Renne in Brittany; studied landscape with Baron Watelet, and figures with Louis David. Also took lessons from Fleischbein (viz.).

After making an abortive attempt to follow his father's watch-making profession, he studied decorative painting with Antonio Modelli Sen. (about 1838) and committed himself definitely to earning his living as an artist. He assisted Pomarede, Mondelli's son-in-law, in painting the "Transfiguration" in St. Patrick's Church, and helped in frescoing the Old Criminal Court ceiling in the Cabildo.

He then studied portrait painting with Julien Hudson and took further lessons from Bigot. From 1841 on, he painted landscapes, birds, animals and fish, and many portraits including 8 judges of the Louisiana Supreme Court and several church dignitaries (see Coulon's biographical notes written for B. A. Wikstrom and preserved in the Louisiana State Museum.) A portrait of Andrew Jackson is in the Jax Brewery made from sketches from life.

Coulon's life span touched the beginning and the end of the nineteenth century. Well rounded in the arts and a superb craftsman, you might say that he ranged from David classicism to Fontainbleau, but with a strong American flavor. His encyclopedic abilities in recording histories of his contemporaries, persons and places, make him an important New Orleanian.

Pauline Coulon, the artist's wife and the two children, Emma and George A. Coulon also were artists of stature. The "nature morte" birds by mother and daughter are superbly realistic.

The vegetable stillife, with the very early can of Salmon bearing the brand "French Market", smacks of Bouillabaise or Courtbouillion.

George A. Coulon generally signed with a cursive "Coulon". His pastels and stillifes are identifiable by a chalky shadow ranging from gray to white.

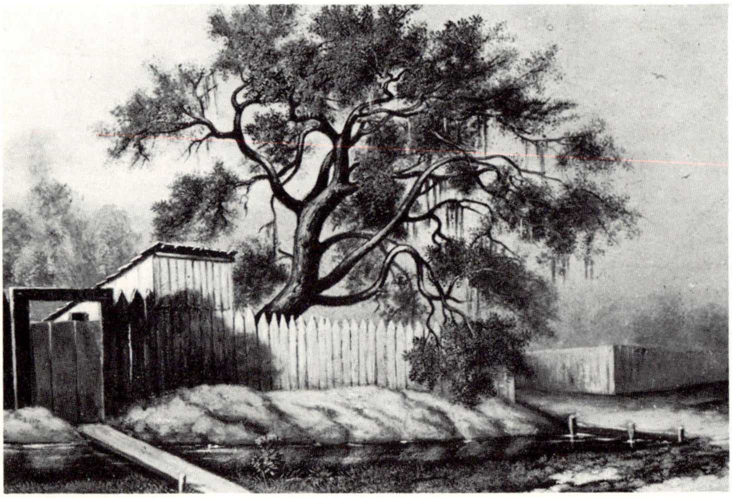

COULON, G. D.
Gentilly Station,
near Hebrews Rest.
9¼" x 12¼"

signed C. D. Coulon '99

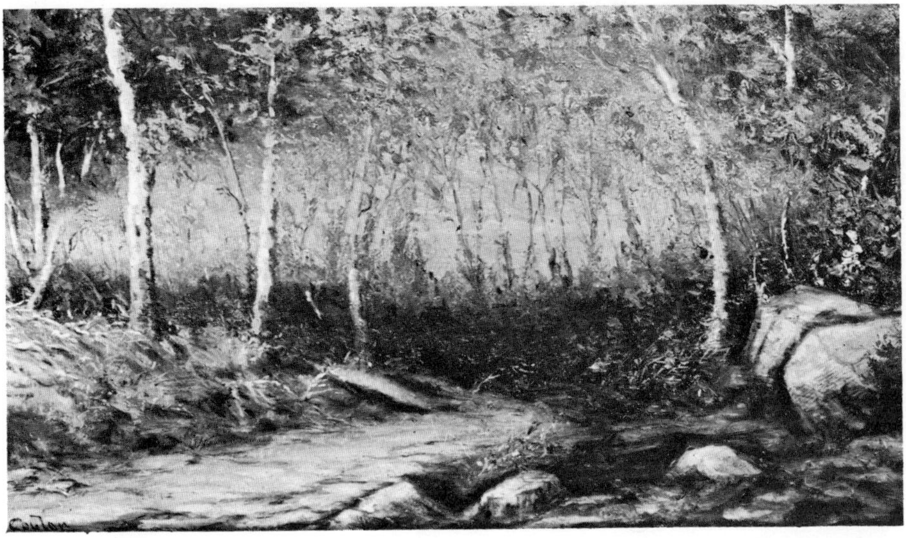

COULON (Son)
Woods Landscape
10" x 17"

signed Coulon

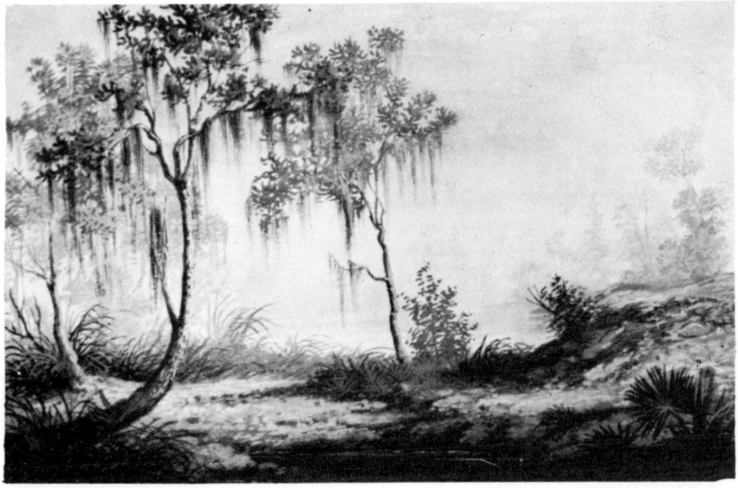

COULON, G. D.
Pond in the Bayou
5" x 7"

signed G. D. Coulon

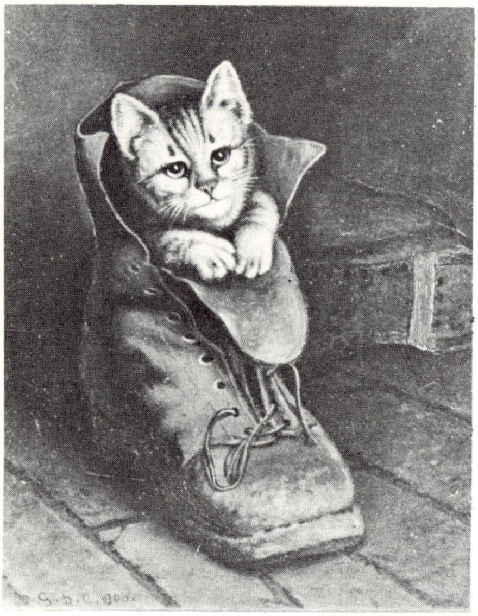

COULON, G. D.
Puss-in-Boots
14½" x 12"
signed G. D. C. 1900

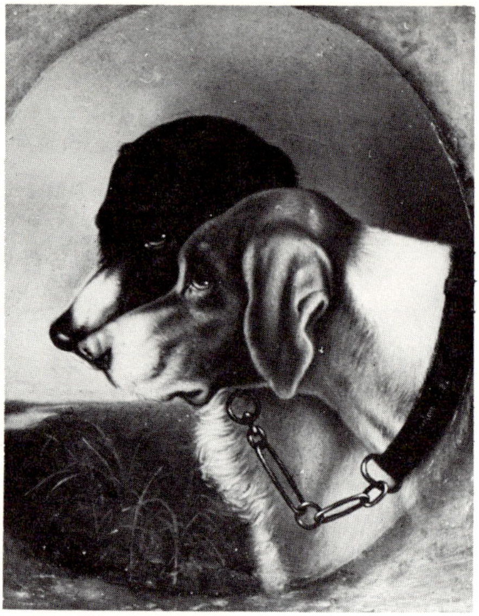

COULON, G. D.
Hunting Dogs
20" x 17"
signed G. D. Coulon 1898

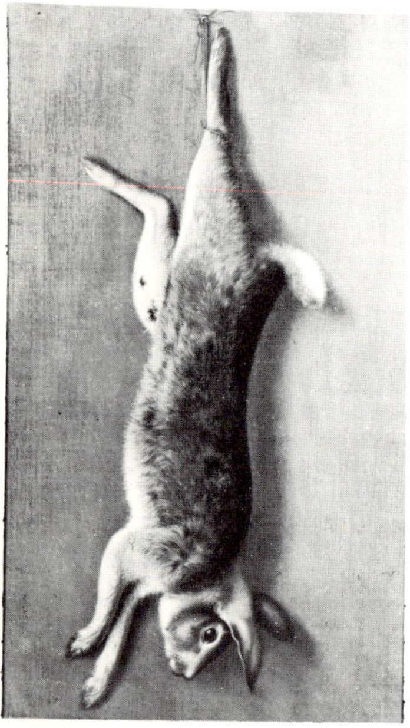

COULON, G. D.
Rabbit
30" x 16" signed G. D. Coulon

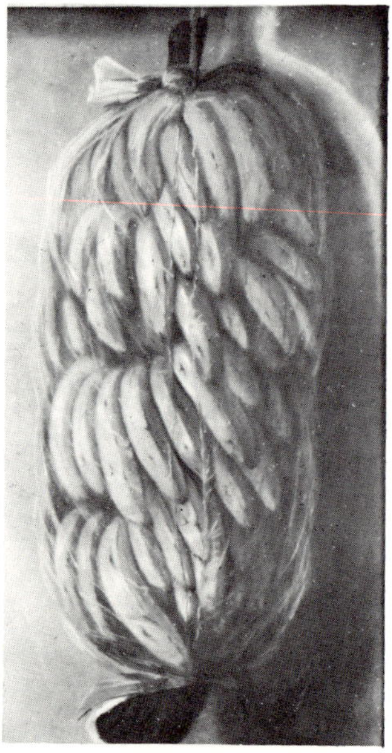

COULON (Son)
Banana Stalk
31½" x 18" signed: Coulon

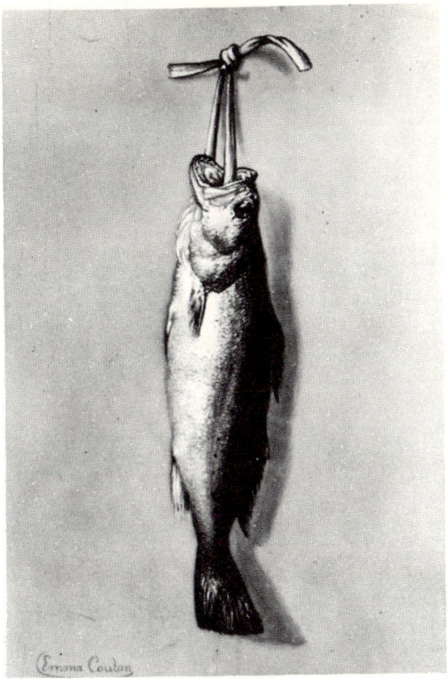

COULON, EMMA
Speckled Trout
21" x 13" signed Emma Coulon

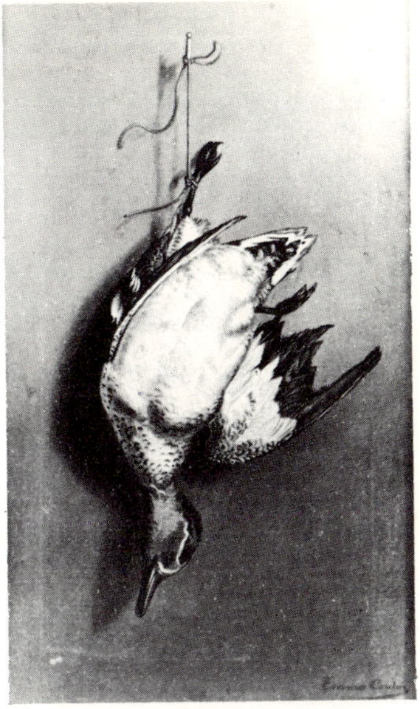

COULON, EMMA
Duck
22" x 13" signed Emma Coulon

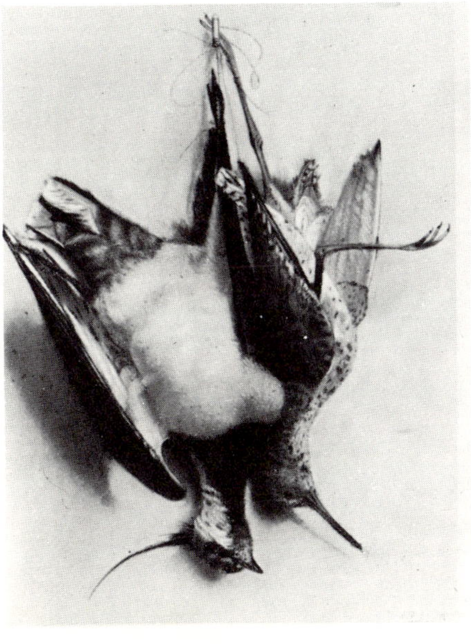

COULON, PAULINE
Snipe and Plover
16½" x 12¼" signed Pauline Coulon

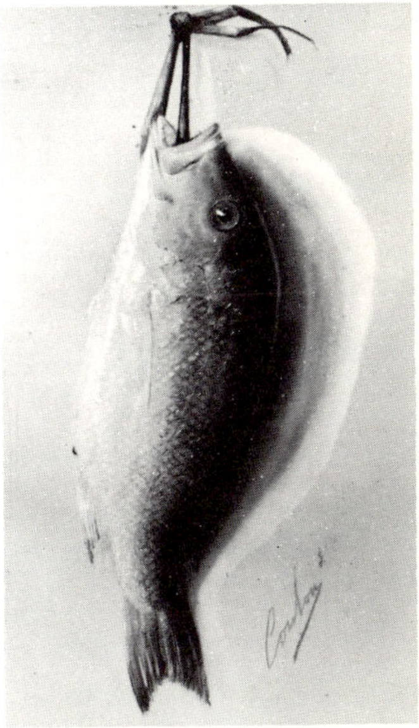

COULON (son)
Red Snapper
29" x 15" signed Coulon

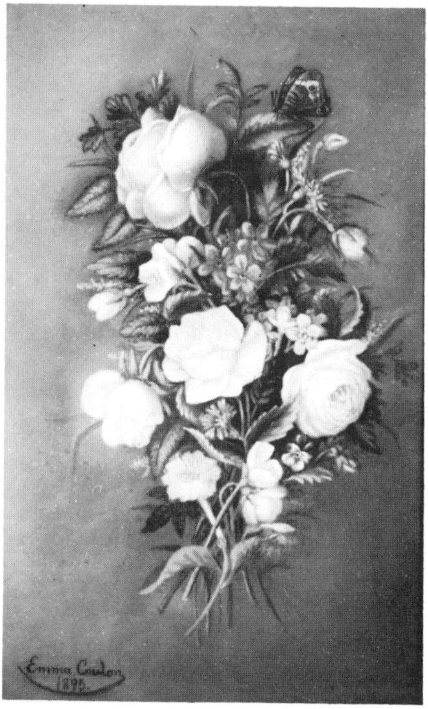

COULON, EMMA
The Bouquet
17½" x 11½"

signed Emma Coulon
1895

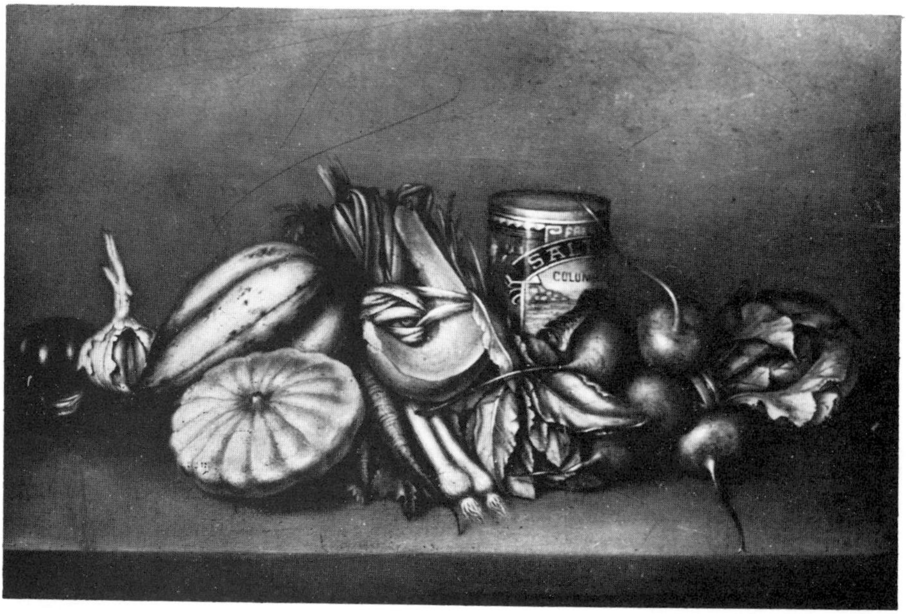

COULON, EMMA
Stillife
15" x 23"

signed Emma Coulon

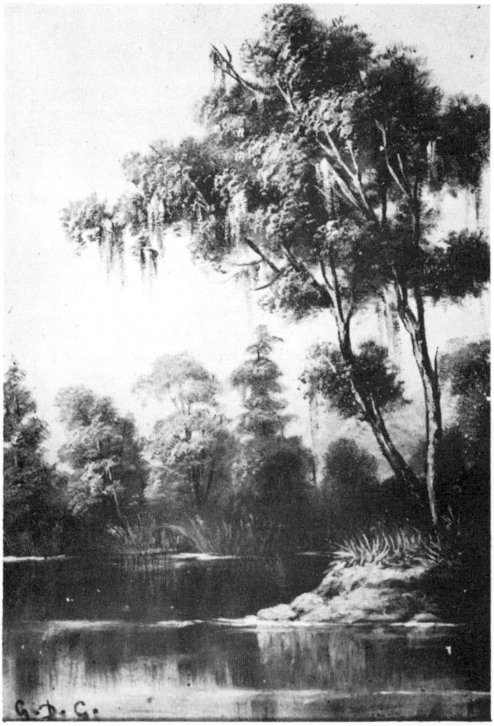

COULON, G. D.
The Bayou
9" x 6"

signed G. D. C.

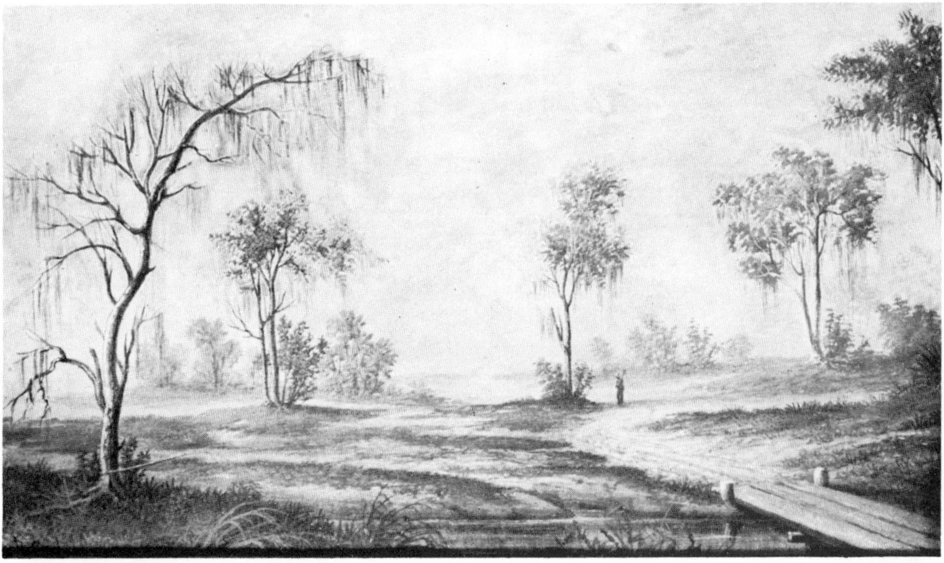

COULON, G. D.
The Path
5½" x 8½"

signed G. D. C.

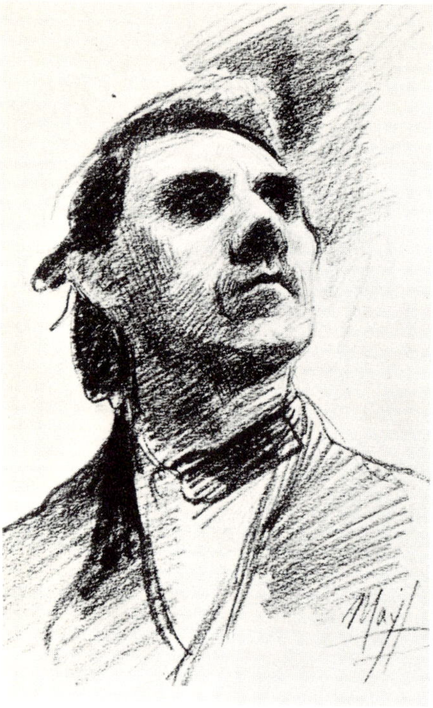

Drawing of Drysdale by R. P. Mayfield

Drysdale, Alexander John

Born 1870 in Marietta, Ga., son of the Rev. Alexander I. Drysdale who was minister to Christ Church in New Orleans in 1885. The young Alexander had his first art lessons from a Miss Haskell, briefly in New Orleans as instructress at the Art Union, later studied under Poincy in New Orleans and at the Art Students League in New York. His teachers in New York were Bryson Burroughs, Chas. C. Curran, Frank Vincent Du Monde. He was a member of the Artists' Association in New Orleans from 1889 on, and joined a turn-of-the-century group of artists in a Sketch Club where he was drawn by Mayfield (see accompanying drawing and under "Mayfield"). Since his death Drysdale's atmospheric landscapes in watercolor and oil have become increasingly popular among residents of Louisiana.

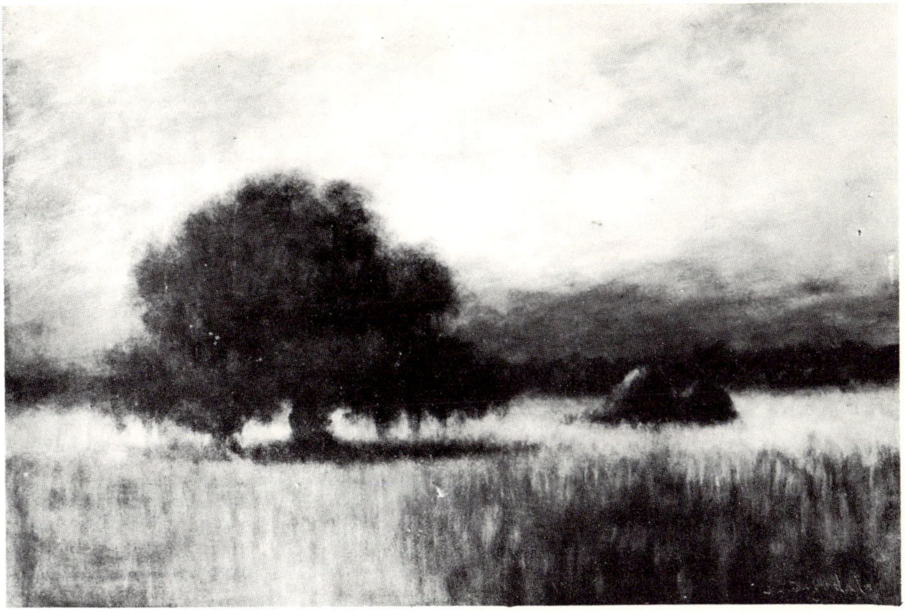

DRYSDALE, A. J. (signed)
Hayfield 18" x 24½"

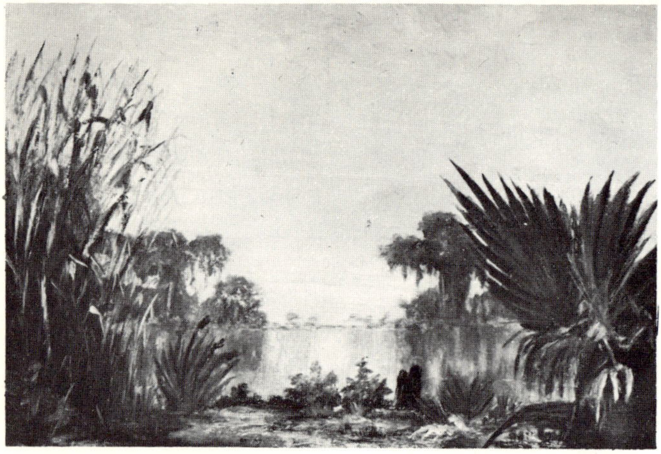

FAURE
Bayou
9¼" x 12"

signed

Two paintings by this unknown painter are in the collection.

Feuille, J. F.

Feuille is one of those artists about whom little is known other than entries in the New Orleans directory and announcements in the New Orleans Bee. These listings date from 1835 to 1841. We place him in New Orleans as early as 1832, however, by the date on the Collection's portrait of Clement Ramos.

We know of only three other signed paintings by this artist, but his style is distinctive enough for us to have made an attribution in the case of the "Portrait of Woman in Red Chair" illustrated here. One other painting in the Collection could also be by Feuille.

We can say with certainty that he emanates from France, but it is likely that he was not well known in his own country. His delineation of character is strikingly alive, but he has difficulties with perspective, and in other ways shows a certain lack of training. His paintings have an indefinable charm, however, which delights their owners.

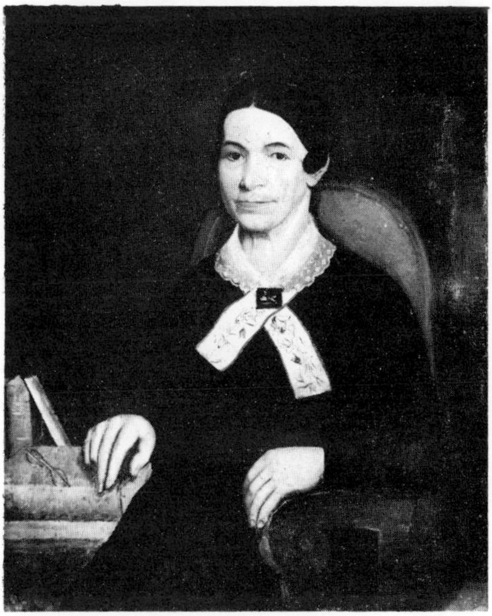

FEUILLE (attrib.)
Portrait of Woman in red chair.
36" x 29"

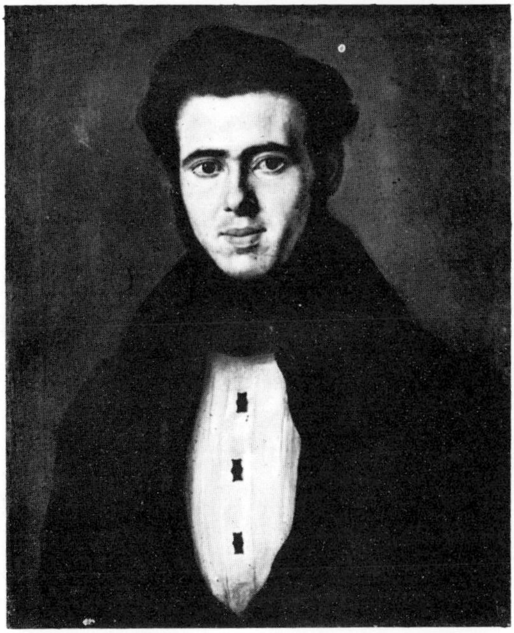

FEUILLE
Portrait of Clement Ramos,
coroner of New Orleans.
signed, 1832

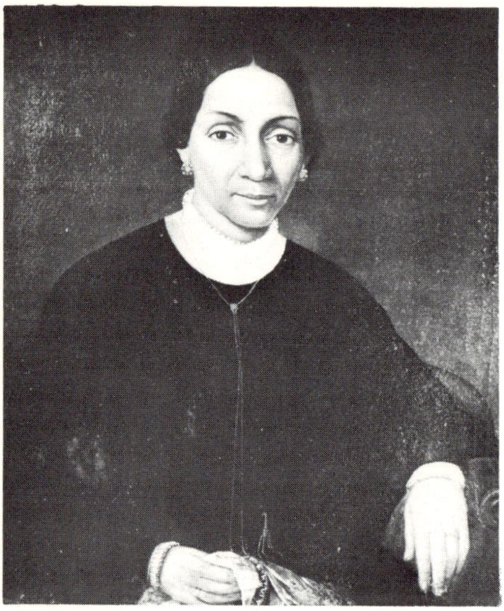

FLEISCHBEIN, FRANCOIS
Portrait of Woman
Oil on canvas, 30" x 25"
signed, "Fleischbein, 1850"

Fleischbein, Francois or Frantz; 1804-1862

A German artist of the Munich school who also studied in Paris under Girardet. Came to New Orleans in 1833, where he was active as a portrait painter and teacher. The New Orleans directory records him from 1840 through 1858, the last listings as a Daguerreotypist and Ambrotypist. Coulon says his sight was very bad in his late years, and that he painted several small historical and mythological pictures as well as portraits.

The unsigned portrait of the younger Marie Laveau, heir to the powers of her mother, the famous Voodoo Queen, was spotted as a Fleischbein by Mr. George Jordan of the Delgado Museum's curatorial staff. A letter in the files of the W. E. Groves Collection from Mr. Fred Brasse, who knew Miss Laveau as his mother's hairdresser, identifies this portrait.

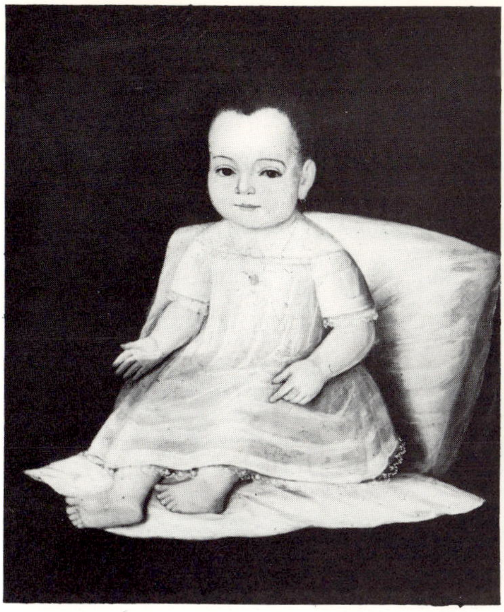

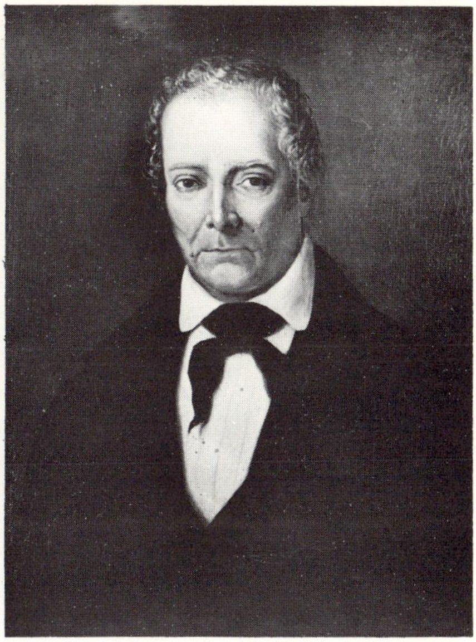

FLEISCHBEIN, F.
Portrait of child
27" x 22"

signed:
Fleischbein 1853

FLEISCHBEIN, F.
Portrait of man, 1850
30" x 25"

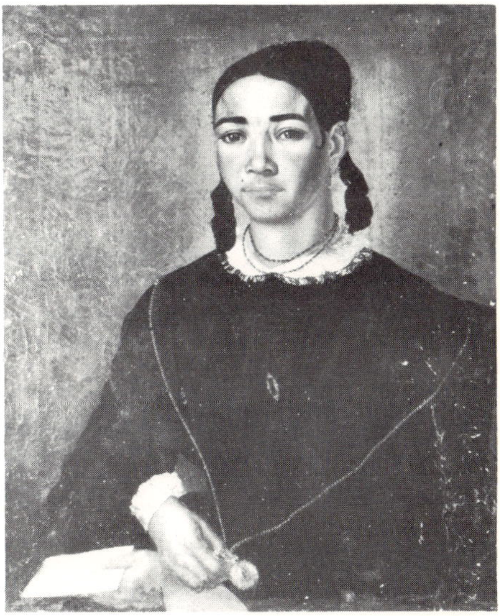

Portrait of Marie Laveau the younger, attributed to Fleischbein.
Oil on canvas, 26½" x 21¼"
Property of the Delgado Museum, gift of Mr. and Mrs. Groves.

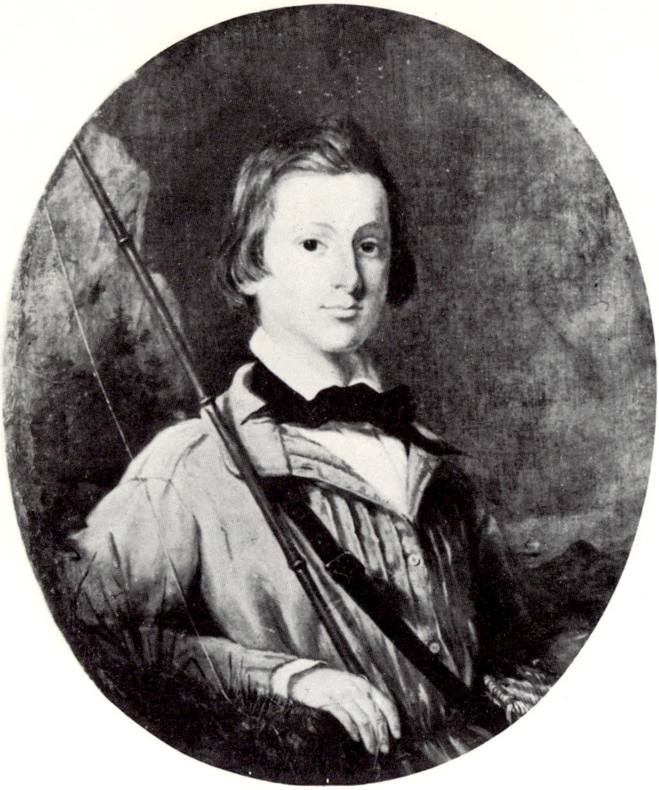

FOWLER, THOMAS TREVOR
The Young Fisherman
31" x 25½" oval

signed:
Thomas Trevor Fowler
1853

Fowler, Thomas Trevor, 1800-1868?

Irish portrait painter born in Dublin, exhibited thirty-five portraits in the Royal Hibernian Academy in Dublin over the years 1830-35. Exhibited in the National Academy at New York in 1838. In 1840 President Harrison and Henry Clay sat for him. Then worked in New Orleans in 1841. Went to Paris 1843 where he studied and returned to New Orleans in 1844 where he worked until 1853. The portrait is dated 1853 and is one of two paintings by this artist in the Groves Collection. It is one of the truly great sporting mid-nineteenth century paintings originating in the South and perhaps the only one where creel, rod and line modify the portrait.

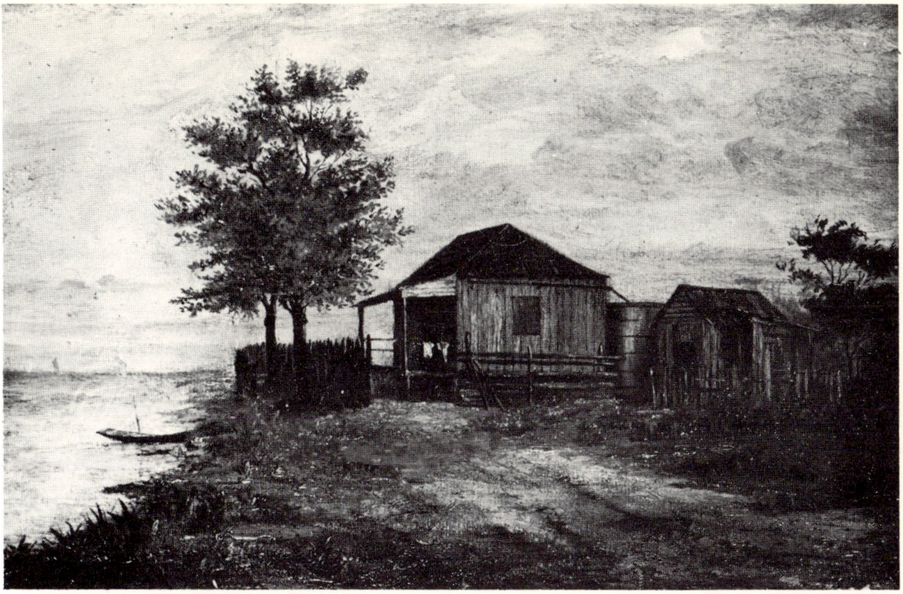

GAMOTIS, ALPHONSE
Cabin on Lake Pontchartrain
10" x 16"

signed Al. Gamotis

Gamotis, Alphonse, c. 1870-1949?

Native New Orleans painter, his style resembles the New Orleans Artists Association's manner, which included Molinary, Walker, Blanchard, Poincy, Livingston, Boyle and others. For many years had a drugstore at Barracks and Rampart St.

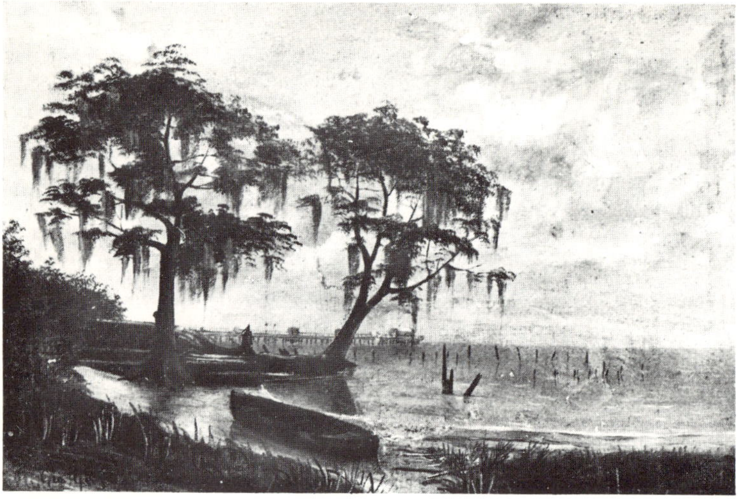

GAY, GEORGE
View near Mandeville
12" x 15"

signed Geo. Gay
'81

Gay, George

Worked in New Orleans in the eighties. Died in 1914.

GENIN, JOHN
View near Biloxi
10" x 14"

signed J. Genin
Biloxi

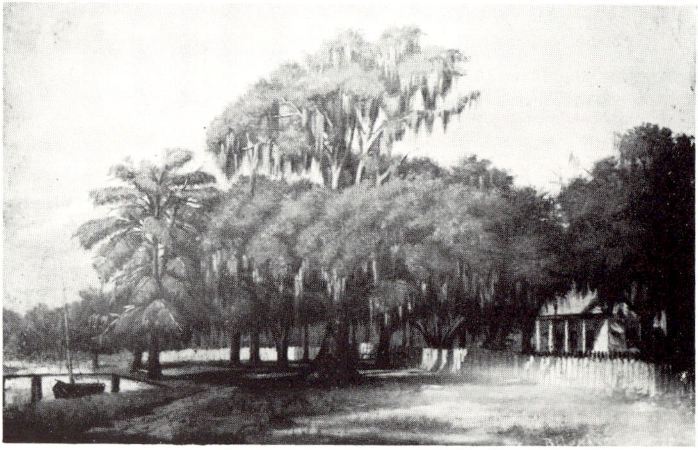

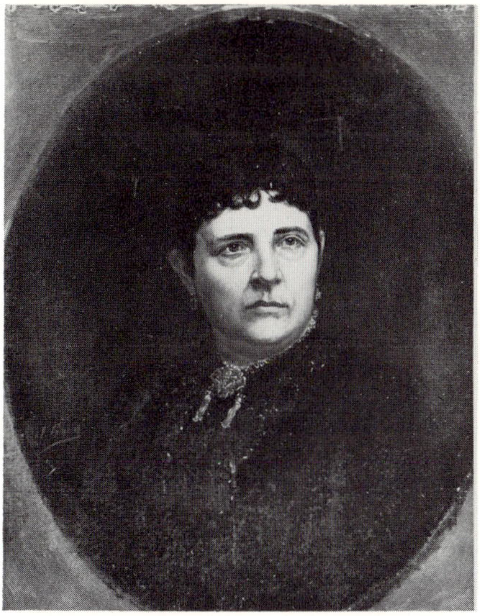

GENIN, JOHN signed J. Genin
Mrs. Joseph Vignes
$27\frac{1}{2}$" x $21\frac{1}{2}$"

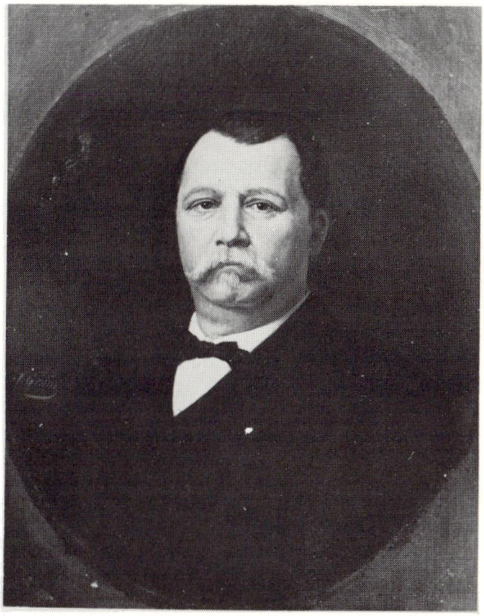

GENIN, JOHN signed J. Genin
Mr. Joseph Vignes
$27\frac{1}{2}$ x $21\frac{1}{2}$"

Genin, John, 1830-1895

Born in France, emerged in New Orleans like a German participle under the ice, in the Carondelet Studio with the painting of "La Jeune Louisiana in 1870". New Orleans Bee. A wonderfully fey maiden emerging in the altogether from a Bayou holding some dripping waterlilies, somewhat Louisiana Bougerau, has been seen by the writer.

He painted many literal portraits which show the influence of the camera, and besides the two portraits, the Groves Collection contains a very able landscape which breathes Louisiana and Mississippi.

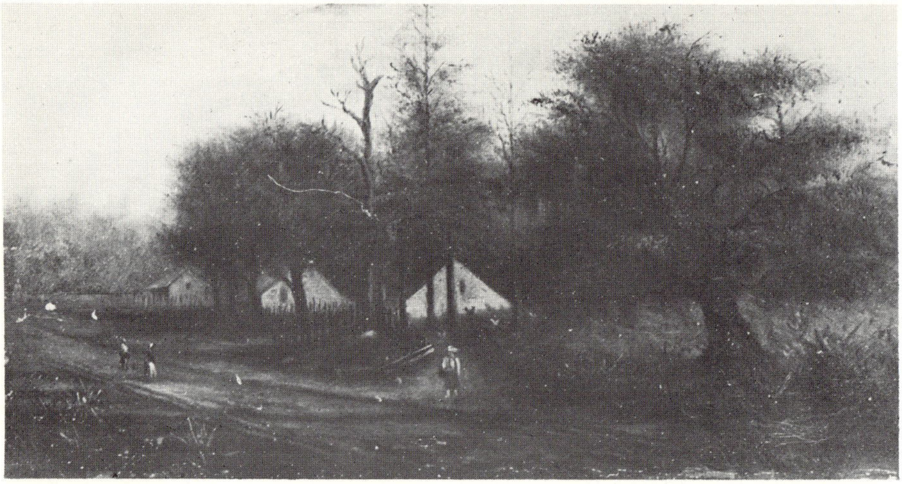

GIRAULT, L. C.
Country Road
11" x 17"

signed

Girault, L. C.

A number of paintings by this artist have found their way into the W. E. Groves Collection. Some are easily confused with those of Ciceri, the scene painter.

Giroux, Charles (Count?)

Listed as a member of the New Orleans Art Association in 1885 and in the city directory as an artist in 1882 and 83, it is conjectured that he studied with Clague though his style is quite distinctive and resembles Persac's particularly in the "River Road", a landscape in the Karolik Collection, now in the Boston Museum. One Clague painting in the Groves Collection is in the Giroux manner. It is known that Blanche Blanchard studied with him and her newspaper biographer refers to him as Count Giroux. A date of 1868 on the Groves' "Marsh Scene with a Heron on a Log" places him in New Orleans at that date. In our opinion, it is questionable to identify him with the C. Giroux, Cotton Broker in the 1870ties and 80ties, or with the architect and surveyor of 1853. The whole Giroux question is shrouded in mystery and perhaps will some day be unravelled. Our patience in the matter has run out.

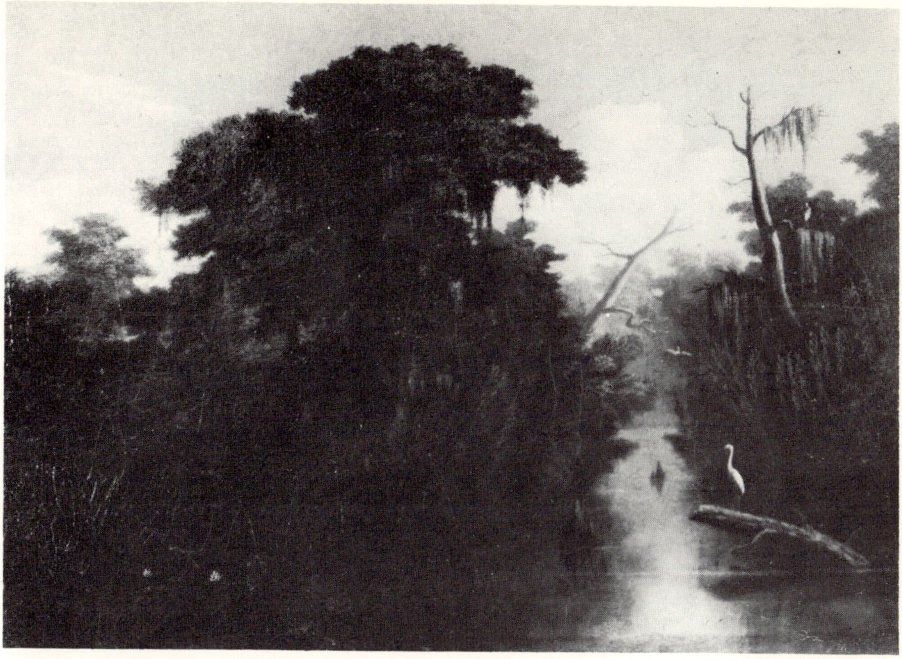

GIROUX, CHARLES
Marsh Scene with Herons on a Log
25" x 29"

signed: C. Giroux 1868

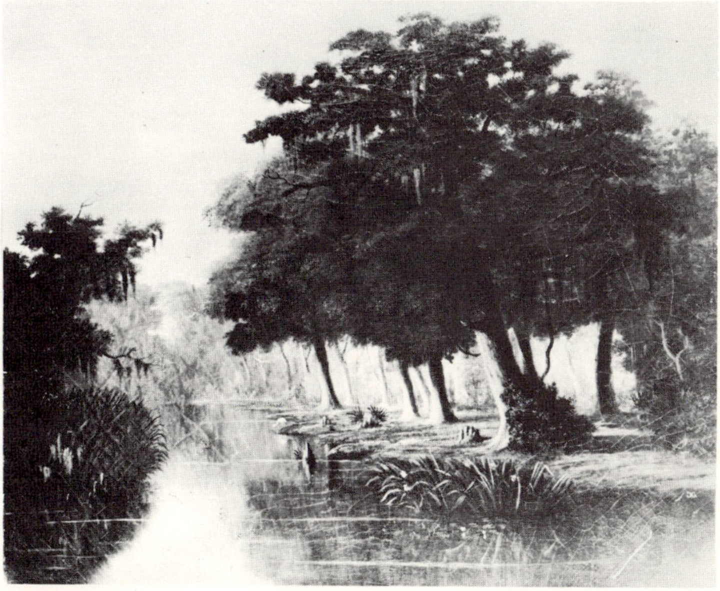

GIROUX, CHARLES
Marsh Scene with Heron on Shore
12½" x 16"

signed with monogram
(reversed C, G combined)

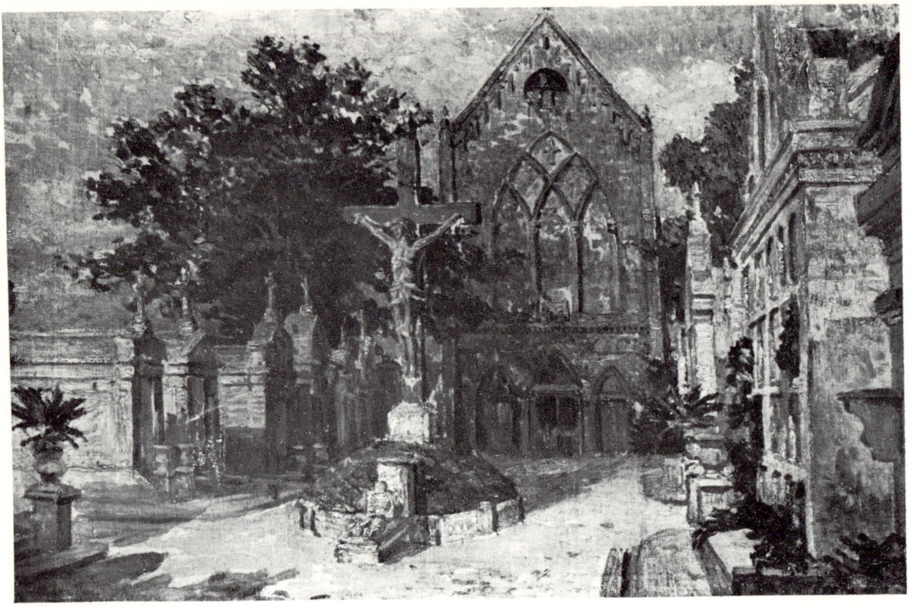

GRAFTON, ROBT. W. signed R. W. Grafton
St. Roch Cemetery Chapel and Campo Santo
21" x 32½"

Grafton, Robert W., 1876-1940?

Landscape, genre and portrait painter, president of the Chicago Society of Artists, studied in England, Holland and France. Worked in New Orleans 1917 to 20. Although of the 20th century, it shows the St. Roch gothic chapel handbuilt personally by Father Thevis in the 1860ties in fulfillment of a vow to the effect that, if his community were spared from yellow fever during the epidemic of 1867, he would build a shrine. Father Thevis even installed the stained glass windows and constructed his own crypt. The community area was designated as Campo Santo by Father Thevis and legend has it that no one in the area contracted the disease. A true mediaevalism in modern times.

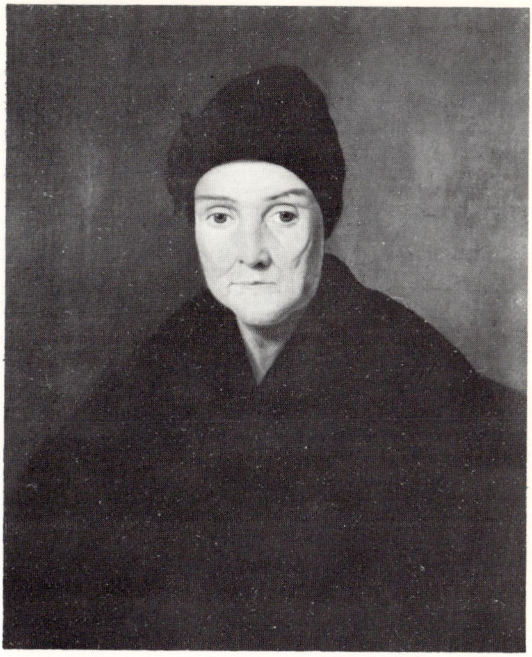

GUENARD, H., after Vaudechamp
(so signed)
Portrait of Mrs. Domingo de Fleistas,
nee Maria Joseph Guenard
32" x 26"

Guenard, Hortier C., 1827- ?

Native of Louisiana of French descent. Is known to have painted portraits in New Orleans 1850-57, where he had a studio on Royal Street. The Choctaw child pictured here was painted ten years after this.

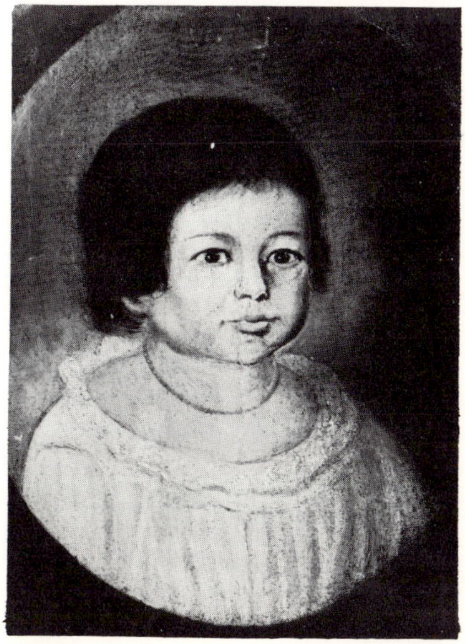

GUENARD, HORTIER
Choctaw Child
15" x 17½"
Signed; H. Guenard
Pinxit 1867

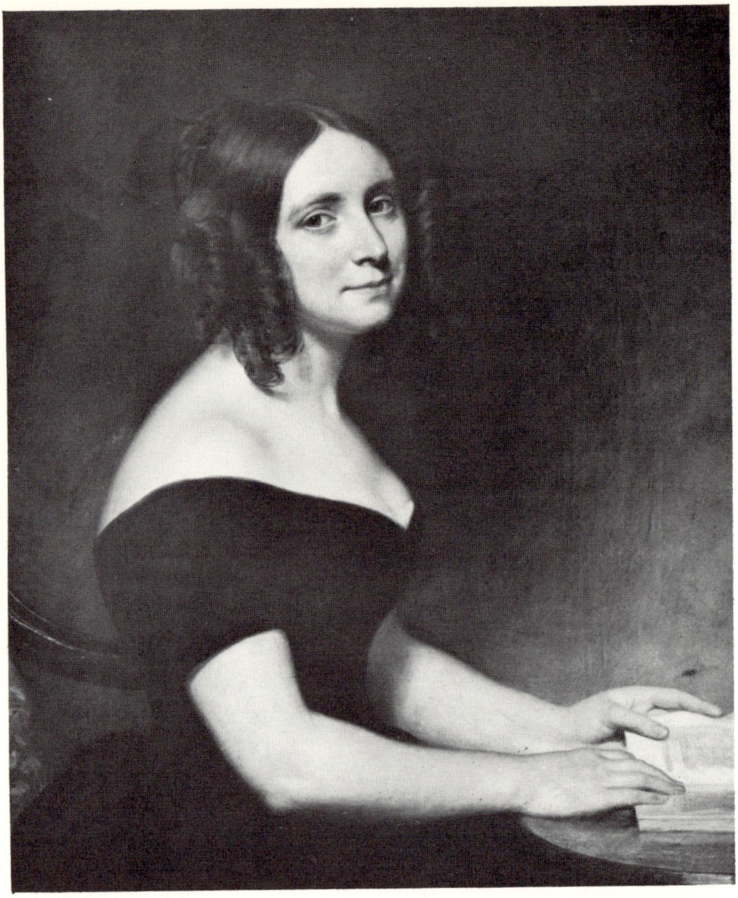

HEALY, G. P. A.
Portrait of a Lady, 32" x 25 5/8"
Courtesy Anglo-American Mus.
Univ. of La., Baton Rouge, La.

signed and dated;
"Geo. P. A. Healy 1845"

Healy, George Peter Alexander, 1813-1894

Eminent American portrait painter of national stature and renown. Born in Boston, he started his career there at age 17, went to France in 1834 to study under Gros, was already internationally known when he returned seven years later. Between 1854 and 1867 he painted most of the prominent statesmen of the time, and members of well-to-do families along the eastern seaboard and the south, as far west as Natchez and New Orleans. He returned to Europe, settling in Rome, but traveled on commissions, even back to the United States. In 1892 he settled in Chicago, where he died two years later.

His most celebrated portrait is that of Lincoln.

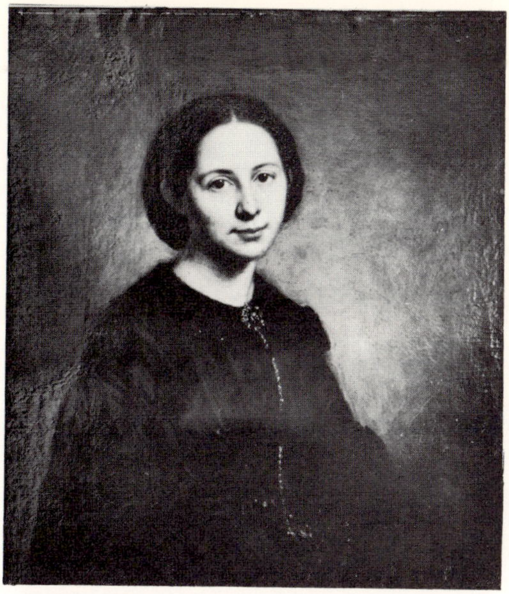

HEALY, G. P. A.
Portrait of a Lady,
Gift of W. E. Groves to the
University of Southwest Louisiana,
Lafayette, La.

Herrman, W.

This painter is not known, but the portrait of Juarez is intriguing because it turned up in New Orleans, and Juarez escaped to New Orleans from Mexico (1853-55).

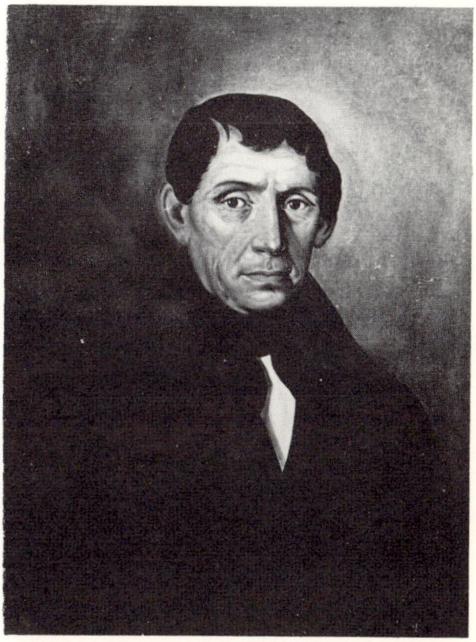

HERRMAN, W.
Portrait of Benito Juarez
23" x 18"
Signed; W. Herrman, Mahler

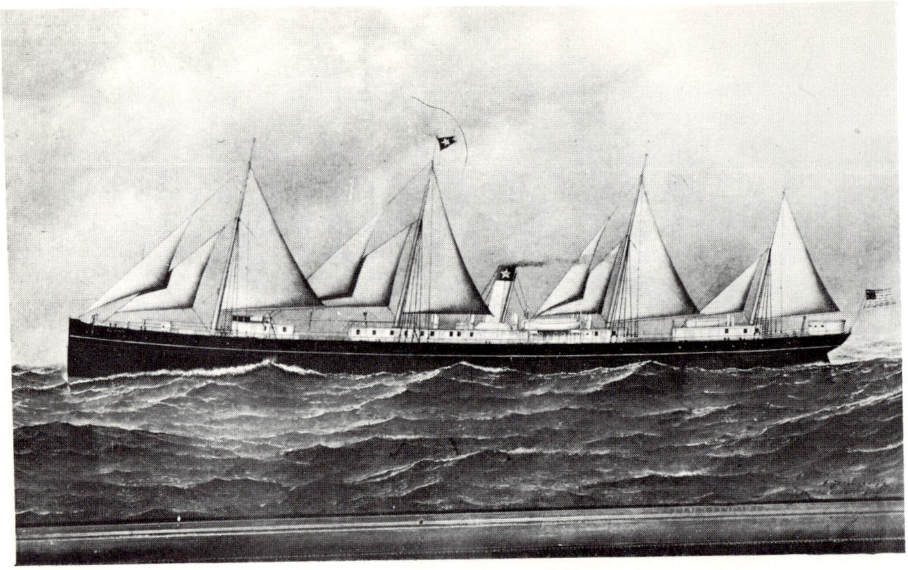

JACOBSEN, ANTONIO
Steamsailer "El Mar", Morgan Line
22" x 30"

signed A. Jacobsen
31 Palisades Ave.
West Hoboken, N. J.

Jacobsen, Antonio, 1860-1920?

Danish sailor painter, probably self trained, lived at 31 Palisades Ave., Hoboken, N. J. The giant tug R. W. Wilmot and the Wilmot Coal Yard appearing in the painting illustrated, does document that Jacobsen came to New Orleans to make the sketch from which the painting was later finished. The Wilmot Coal Yard was located in Algiers directly across from the Canal Street Landing. From the Wilmot family comes further information; that the other tug, originally named the *Robert W. Wilmot*, then changed to the *Potomac;* helped to tow the drydock *Dewey* to Manila, giving rise to a sea story of hair-raising adventure (Scribners Magazine, May 1907, Vol. XLI No. 5). The *R. W. Wilmot* particularly was the most powerful steamtug of its time and still lies at the foot of Walnut Street, New Orleans, in the Bisso Yard. Jacobsen did another painting in the collection, the Morgan Liner "El Mar", a steam sailer.

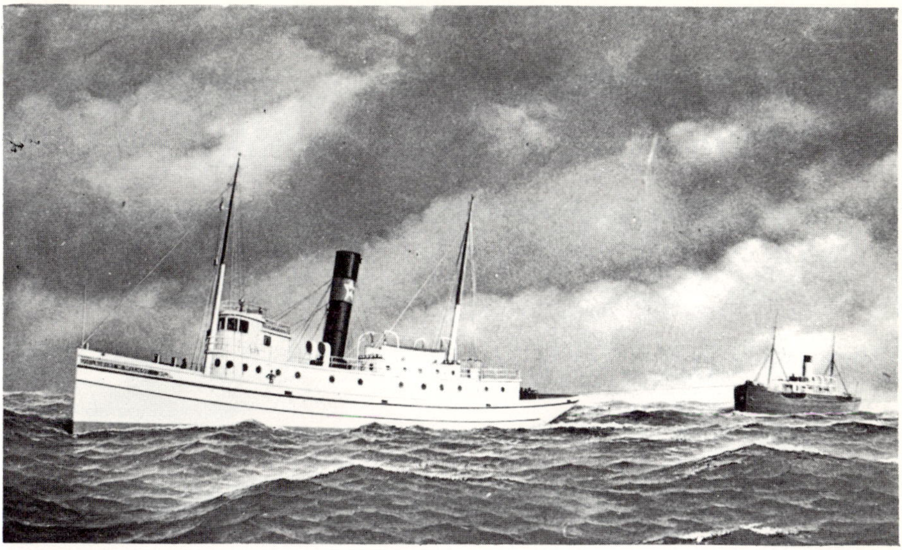

JACOBSEN, ANTONIO
Robert W. Wilmot, later named the Potomac
30" x 49½"

signed A. Jacobsen 1898
31 Palisades Ave.
Hoboken, N. J.

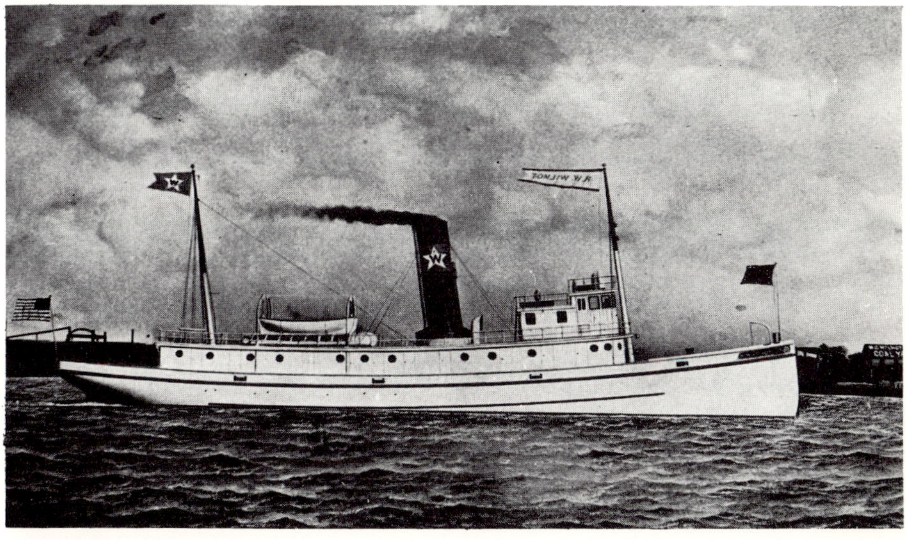

JACOBSEN, ANTONIO
R. W. Wilmot
30" x 49½"

signed Antonio Jacobsen
1899

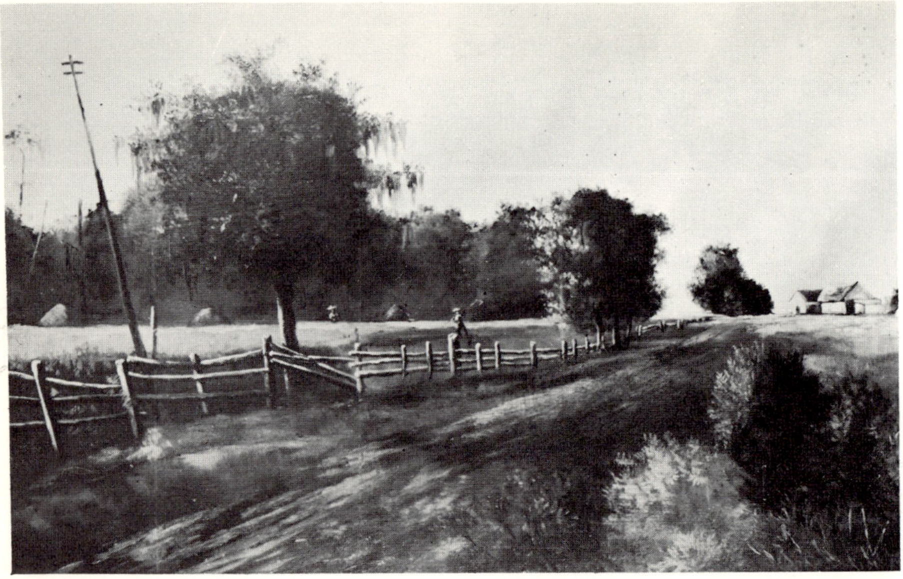

JULIO, E. B. D. FABRINO — signed
Louisiana Road
20" x 30"

Julio, E. B. D. Fabrino, 1843-1879

This is a painter whose work would be much better known had his career been a little longer, for his mature work is of the highest quality. He was born in the island of St. Helena of an Italian father and Scotch mother, according to Mantle Fielding's Dictionary. (The St. Louis City Art Museum catalogue of the exhibition "Mississippi Panorama 1949", says a Spanish father in the employ of the British government.) He was educated in Boston, and in 1864 went to St. Louis where he worked as an artist. In the late 60's or early 70's he changed his residence to New Orleans where he lived most of the rest of his life except for a year's study in Paris with Leon Bonnat. He contracted tuberculosis and died at the age of thirty-six in Kingston, Georgia.

He painted some fine landscapes and genre paintings and a few historical subjects, notably "The Meeting of Gen. Lee and Stonewall Jackson", from which a print was made. Julio made two copies of this painting, one owned by the Washington Artillery, New Orleans, the other by the University of Louisiana, Baton Rouge.

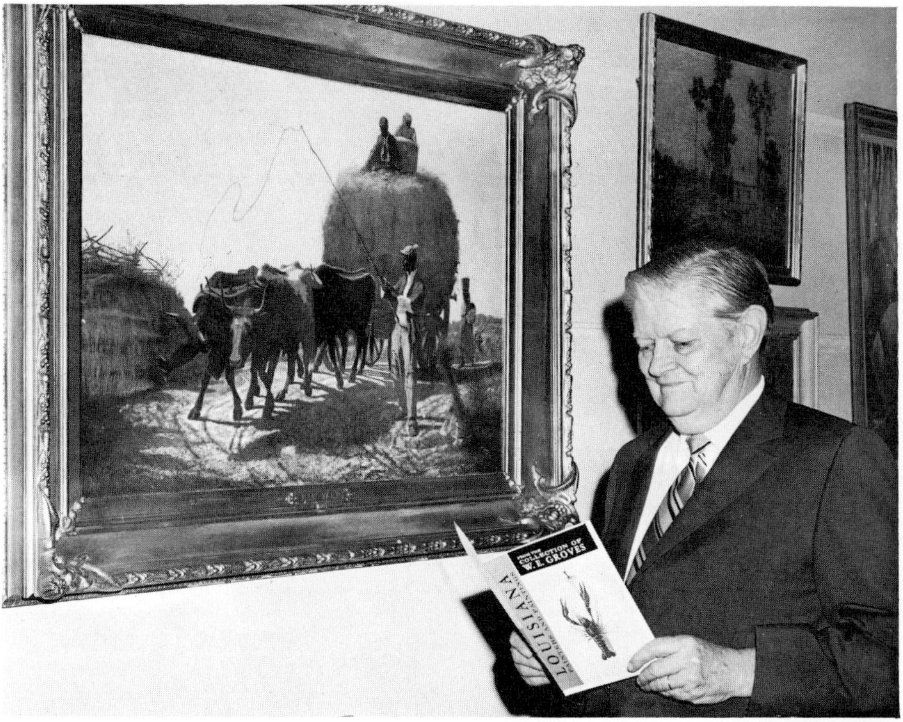

photo by A. P. Vidacovich for the Times-Picayune

Mr. Groves in the Gallery of his Collection beside the painting called "Haw-Yar" by E. B. D. FABRINO JULIO, reproduced in color on the back of this catalogue. The painting is signed; "Julio, New Orleans, La., 1871", size, 29½" x 44".

Besides the two examples of his work illustrated here, the Collection also contains one other signed Louisiana landscape, and formerly owned one called "Hay Wagon", exhibited in 1969 in the Anglo-American Museum, Louisiana State University, Baton Rouge, La., and illustrated in the catalogue titled "The Louisiana Landscape".

Of particular interest is the very effective artistic device of backlighting in the "Haw-Yar" with the drama of resultant shadow pattern. It places him strongly beside the immortals such as Winslow Homer, and one regrets that he did not have a few more years to develop these ideas. His interest in genre subjects might have given us more truly great paintings of southern life.

LANSOT, A. D.
Portrait of Mme. Theo. Ballard
35" x 28"

not signed, but family
tradition credits Lansot

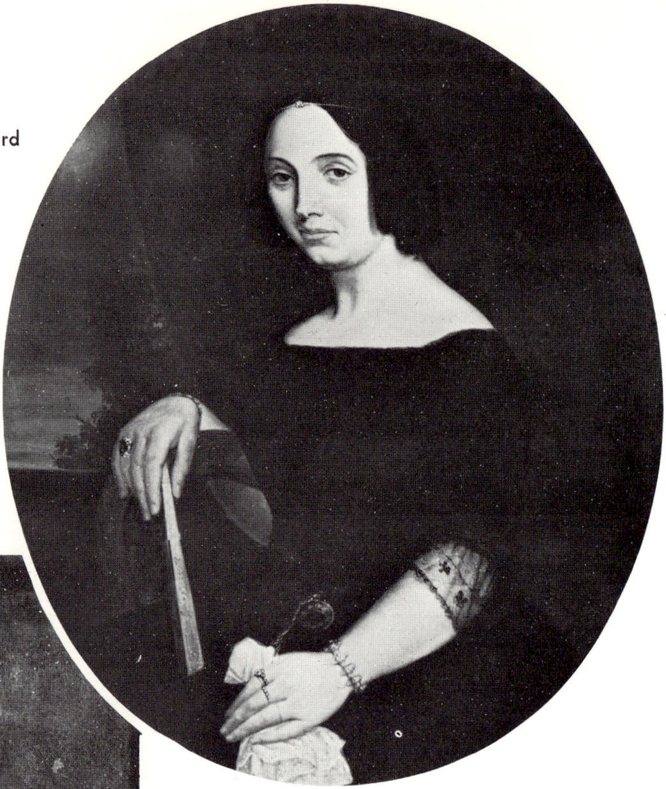

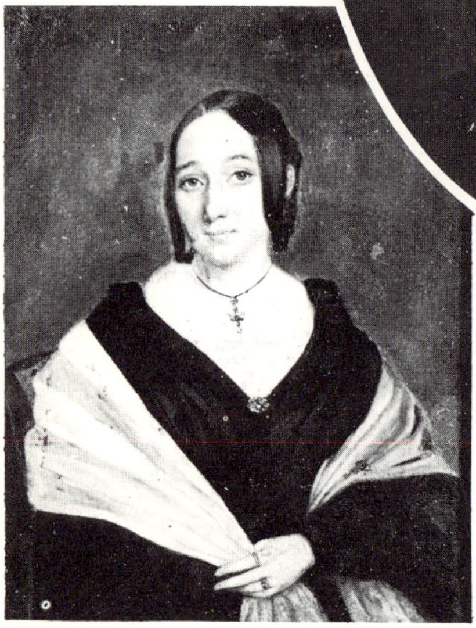

LANSOT, A. D.
Portrait
13" x 9¾"
signed; Lansot, 1842

Lansot, A. D. (died c. 1850)

Coulon says that in the beginning of the 40's Vaudechamp and Lansot were the leading portrait painters in Louisiana. Dr. Cline places him in New Orleans from 1834 to about 1850. In 1843 he was at 165 Royal, in '46 at 33 Toulouse.

He was known as a portrait, miniature and landscape painter, and advertised himself as a restorer and as making daguerreotypes. It was once suspected that he was the first to make daguerreotypes in New Orleans, but it now seems fairly well established that honor belongs to Jules Lion.

An interesting aspect of the two portraits illustrated is the detailed recording of the jewelry of the period.

Laughabaugh, C. O. (dates unknown)

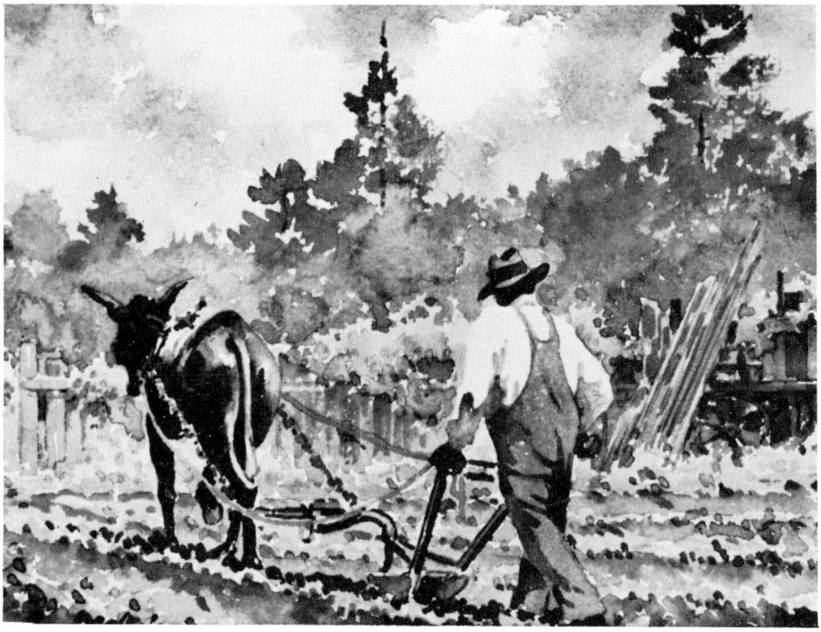

LAUGHABAUGH, C. O.
Git along Mule
6" x 7"

Signed: C. O. Laughabaugh

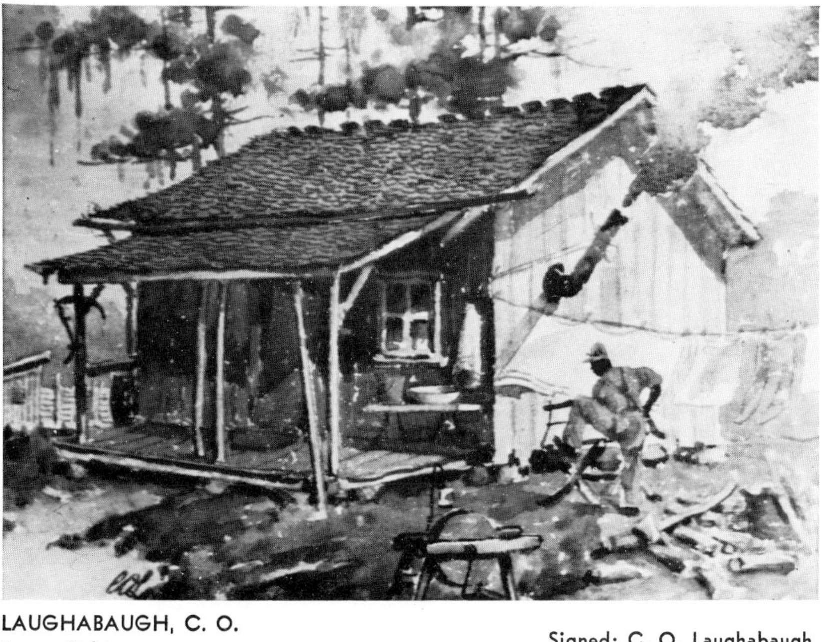

LAUGHABAUGH, C. O.
Bayou Cabin
6" x 7"

Signed: C. O. Laughabaugh

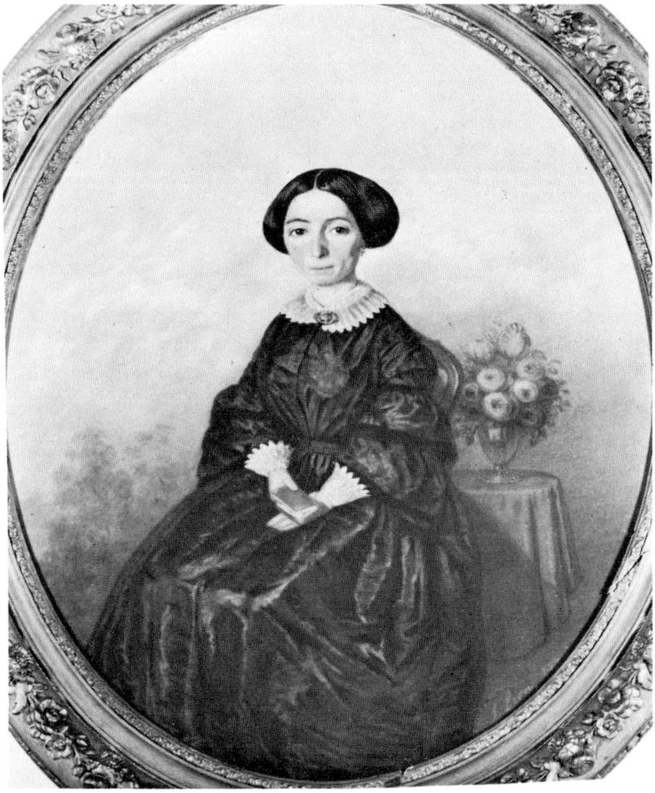

LION, JULES: Pastel portrait 28" x 23"
Courtesy Univ. of S. W. Louisiana
Gift of W. E. Groves

signed:
J. Lion, 1852

Lion, Jules, 1816-1866

French portrait and miniature painter, lithographer and one of the first daguerreotypists in the United States. A free man of color according to the 1851 New Orleans City directory. Producer of pastels of fine quality. Advertised in the New Orleans Bee March 14, 1840, an exhibition of daguerreotypes and drawings. Advertised further in 1843 "apparatus for taking Daguerre portraits of very large dimensions or brooch size. Daguerre announced the first exhibition of his invention January 15th, 1839. On August 21st, 1839 the book "Historique et Description des procedes du Daguerreotype" appeared in Paris under the imprint A. Giroux et Cie, containing seventy-nine pages of instructions and detailed scale drawings of the required apparatus. However the Groves Collection contains a lithograph by Lion dated New Orleans 1837 which has the slight stiffness of a daguerreotype. Had Lion come to America with knowledge of the process before 1937 or had he constructed the apparatus from the Giroux book? He did a large photograph (daguerreotype) of the St. Louis Cathedral in the early 1840ties and a lithograph also.

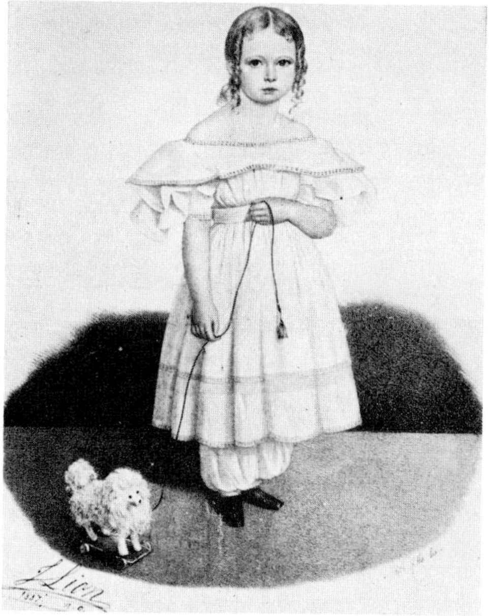

LION, JULES
Lithograph of Child with Toy Dog
$11\frac{1}{2}$" x 9"

signed: J. Lion,
1837, N. O.

LION, JULES: Two examples of his lithographic portraits. He did lithographs of many Louisianians, including the judges of the Supreme Court.

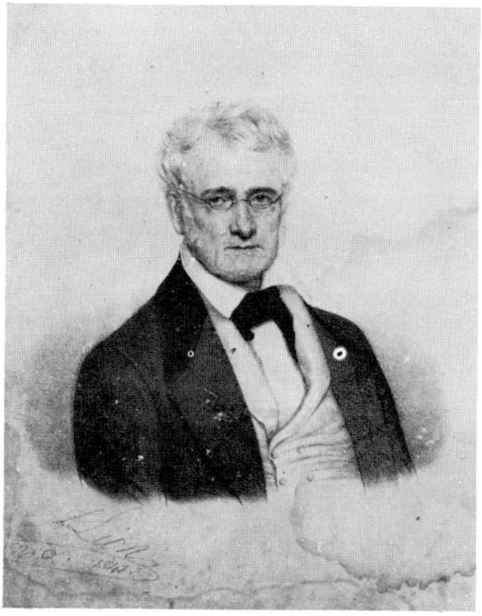

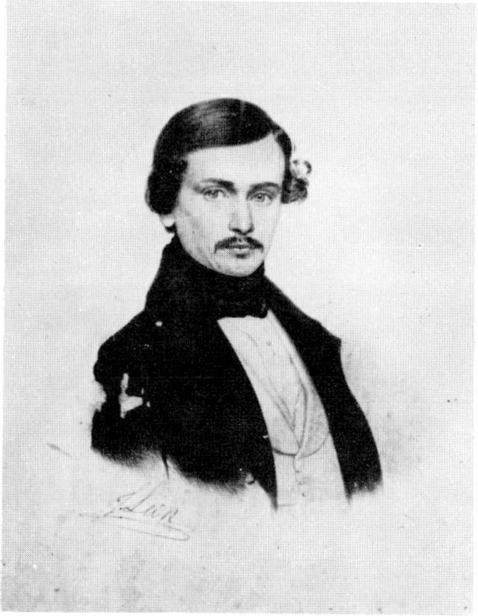

Lion was highly praised in the New Orleans Bee, November 25, 1843: "J. Lion is prepared to take likenesses by the Daguerreotype or Lithographic process, at his rooms, #3 St. Charles Street. Mr. Lion is an artist of superior merit of which anyone can convince himself by an examination of the specimens before the office door."

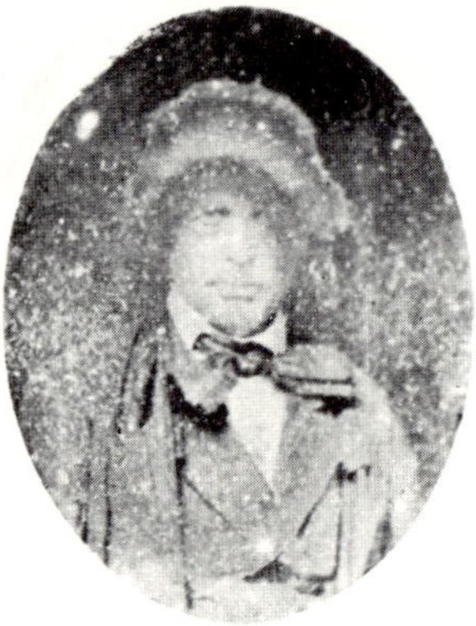

Daguerreotype with "Lion" scratched into the metal. Is it by Lion or a likeness of Lion?

Livingston, Edward

A business man of New Orleans who painted as an avocation "poetic landscapes, pleasing in color, both in oil and water colors, during the 80's and 90's" (Dr. Cline; Art and Artists in New Orleans during the Last Century, 1922). Closely associated with Marshall Smith in the Art Union.

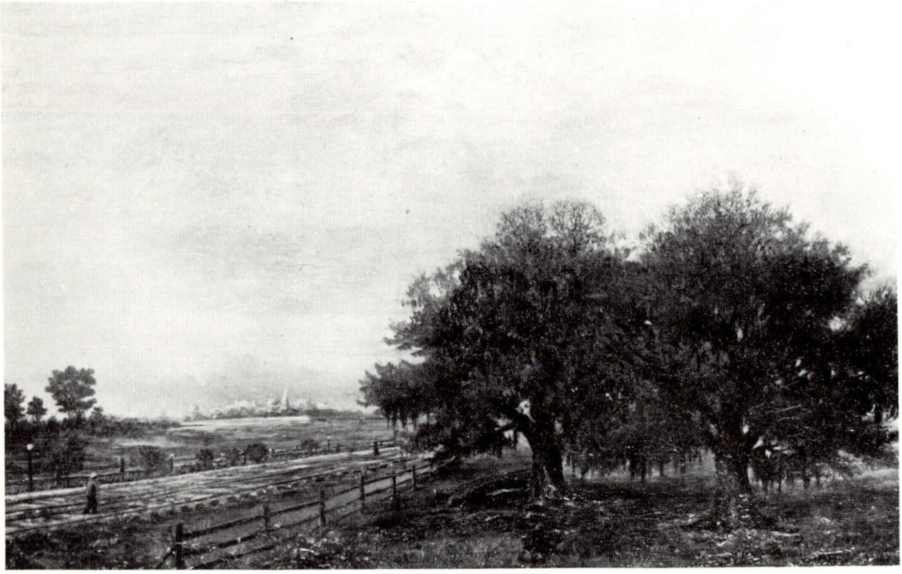

LIVINGSTON, EDWARD
"Walking the Tracks"
12" x 18"

signed: E. Livingston

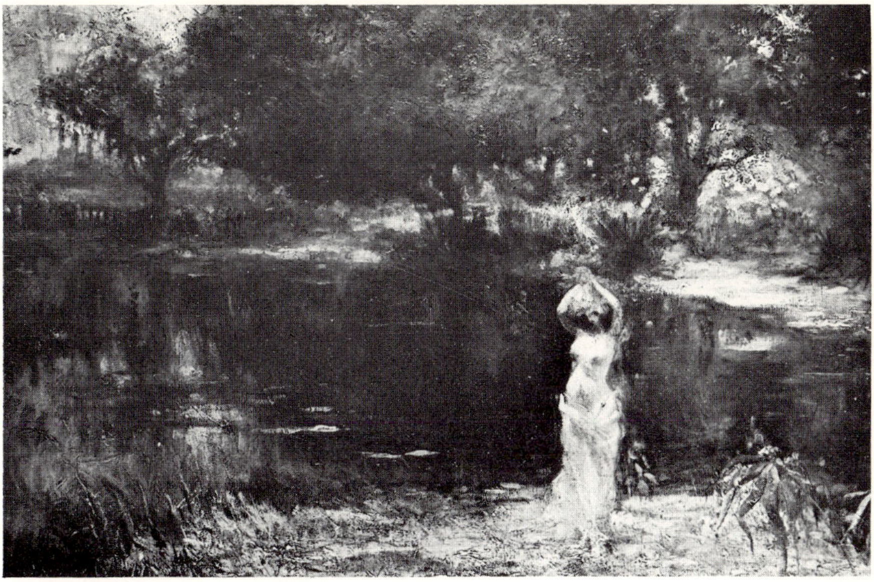

MAYFIELD, R. B. signed: "Mayf"
Nymph by the Lake, 20" x 24½"
(locale, Audubon Park, N. O.)

Mayfield, Robert Bledsoe, 1869-1934

Born in Illinois, lived in Europe as a boy, at school in Germany and Switzerland. Received his art training at the St. Louis Academy of Art, later to become part of Washington University, and at the Julien Academy in Paris. Among his teachers were Jules Lefebvre, Benjamin Constant and L. Oliver Merson. After serving a short apprenticeship as artist for the St. Louis Post Dispatch, he came to New Orleans (1891) as Associate Editor on the Times-Democrat. Was the author of the paper's Art and Music reviews. Was for many years active in the art life of the city.

As a member of a Sketch Club formed around the turn of the century, he has left us drawings and caricatures of other members of the club. His etchings are particularly sensitive records of New Orleans places and people. The one shown here is of Dr. Cline who was such an influence in the early stages of the formation of Mr. Groves' Collection. This etching, as well as the drawings made at the "Sketch Club" are gifts to the Collection by Marcia Mayfield Matthews and Sally Matthews, daughters of Mr. Mayfield.

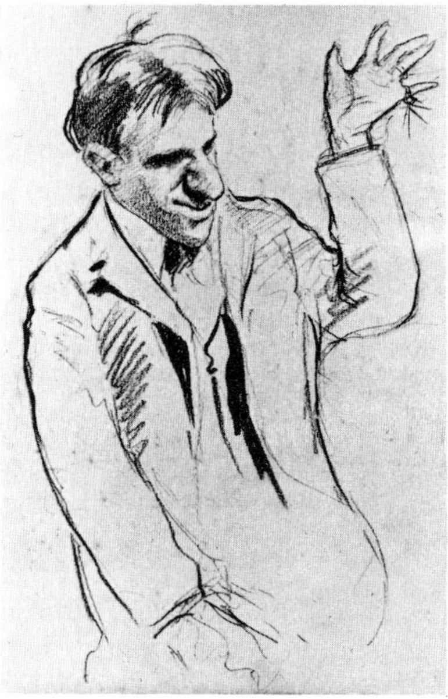

John Pemberton (caricature)

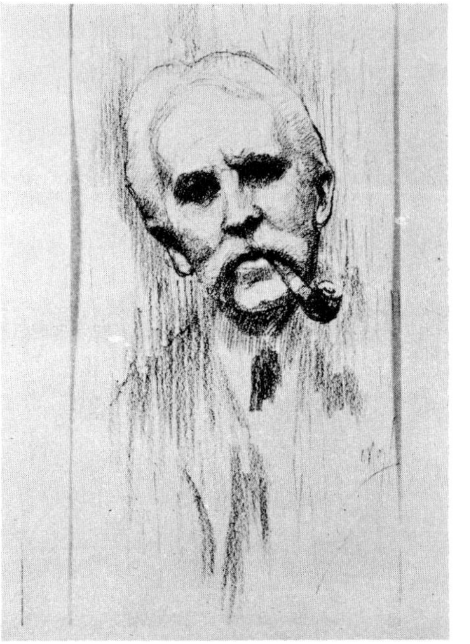

Patrick Westfeld

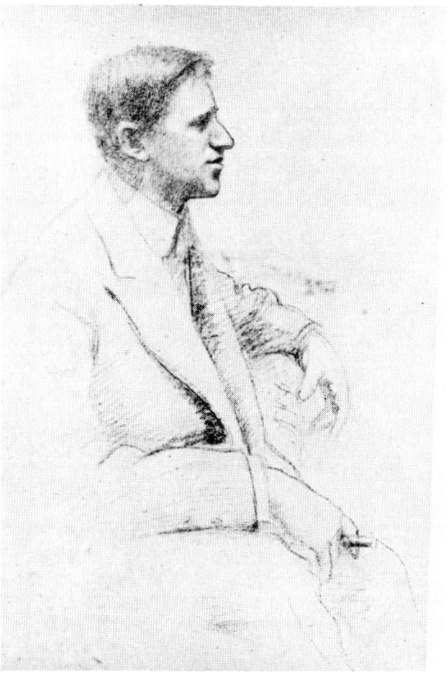

John Pemberton

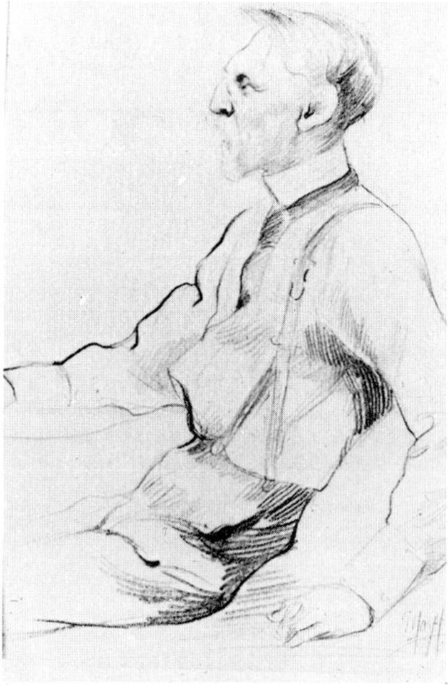

William Woodward

MAYFIELD, R. B.: Members of the "Sketch Club" (pencil)

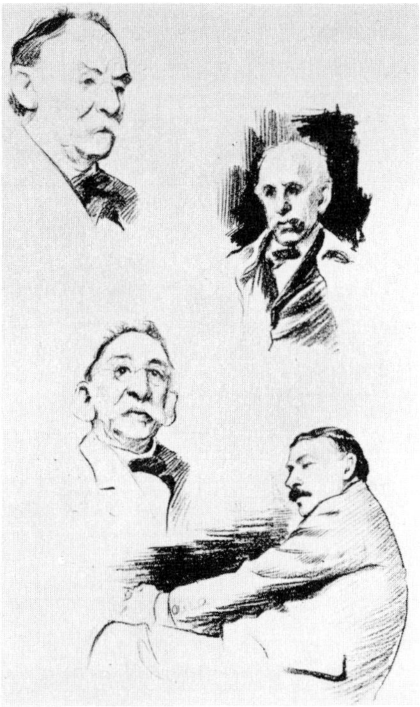

A. Molinary — Patrick Westfeld
A. Molinary — C. W. Boyle

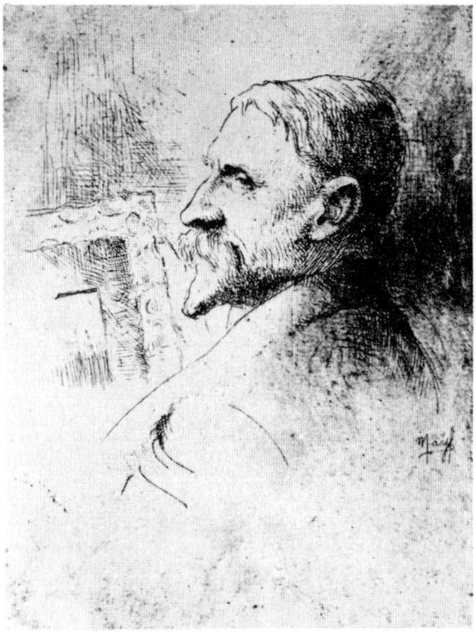

Dr. I. Cline (etching)

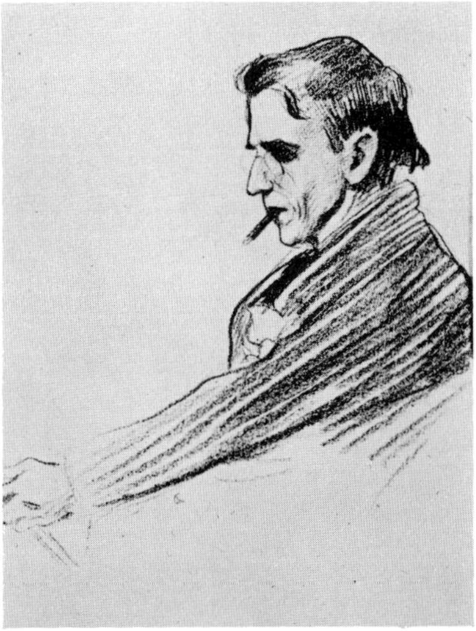

A. J. Drysdale

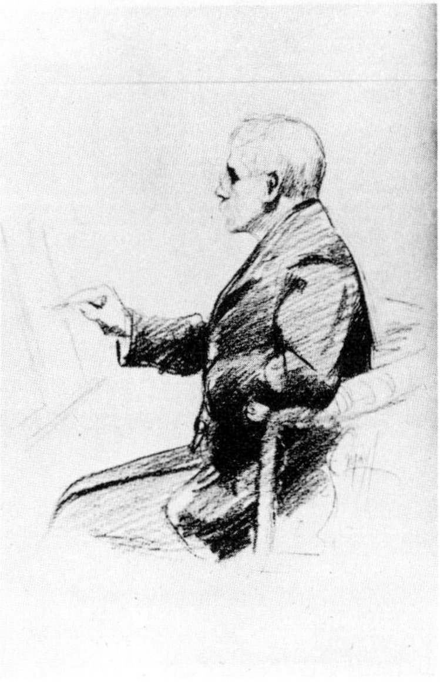

Patrick Westfeld

MAYFIELD, R. B.
Sketches done of members of the "Sketch Club", and an etching of Dr. I. Cline, art collector, of hurricane-prediction fame.

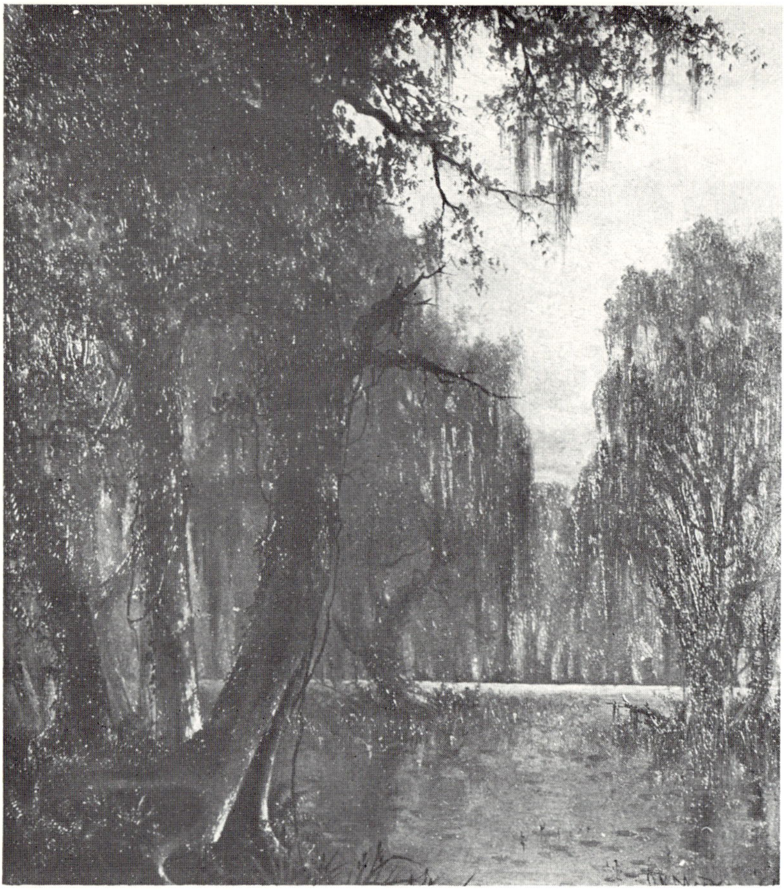

MEEKER, JOSEPH RUSLING
Acadian Land
14½" x 16½"

signed J. R. Meeker 83

Meeker, Joseph Rusling, 1827 ?

Born in Newark, N. J., painted throughout the South, painted on the Bayou Teche and the "Land of Evangeline" and finally settled in St. Louis.

> "No man has lived well, until he has breathed the soft air of our great swamps, fragrant and mouldy at the same time, gloomy at one point and shafted with sunlight at another, a region of magic."

F. Gerstaecker, Jagd und Streifzuge 1845.

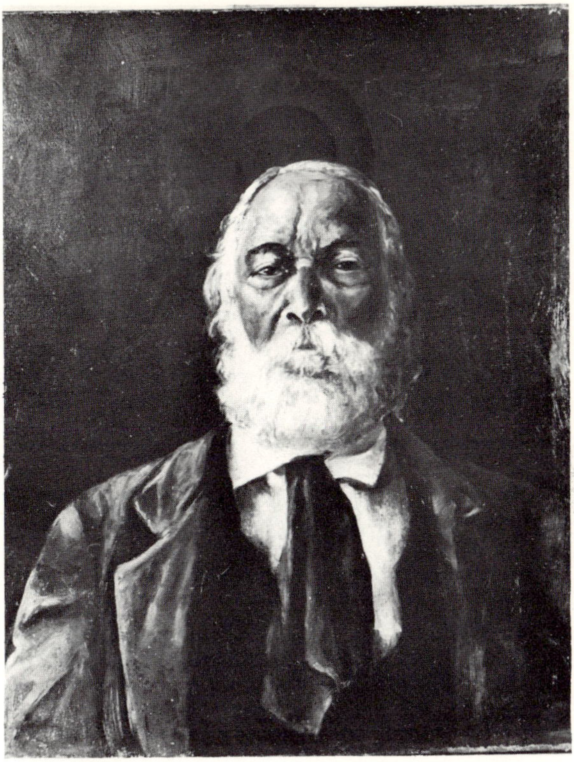

MILTENBERGER, LUCIA
Portrait Study
27" x 22"

Miltenberger, Lucia, 1871-1955

The Miltenberger name is associated with a famous triple house at 902-910 Royal Street in New Orleans. The widow of Dr. Christian Miltenberger, physician at the Battle of New Orleans in 1838, replaced the original modest house with three dwellings at a recorded cost of $29,176 in which her three sons, Gustave, Aristides and Alphonse lived.

Lucia, largely self-trained, travelled extensively in Europe, spending her summers wandering with her cousin, the first American Princess of Morocco. A number of her "tapestry paintings", popular at the turn of the century, are extant. The portrait is perhaps of an old family retainer and reflects dignity and balanced pride. Like Walker's paintings, it recognizes Man, not Race.

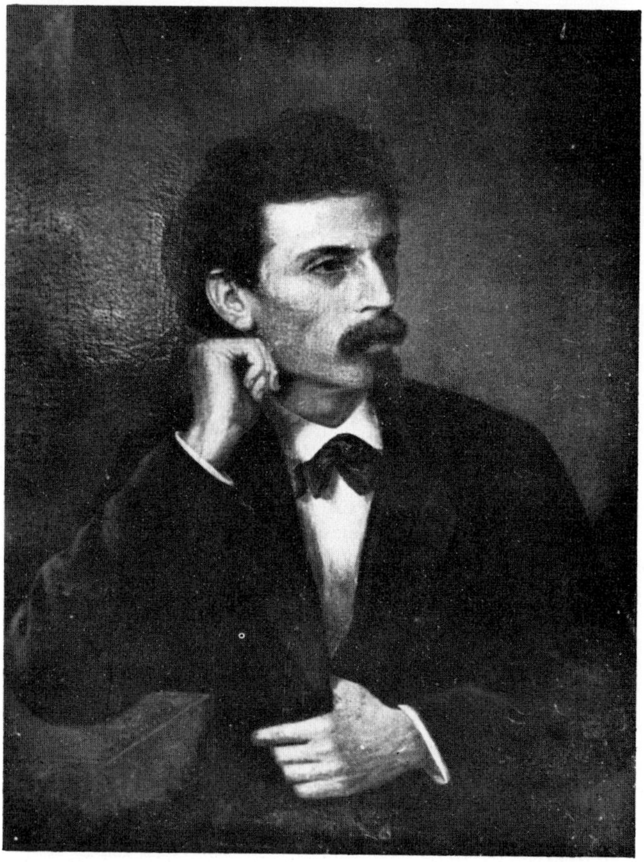

Moise, Theodore Sidney
Portrait of a Man
36" x 29"

signed Moise 1869

Moise, Theodore, Sidney, 1806-1883

Born in Charleston, S. Carolina. Came to New Orleans in 1842. Very able portraitist. Painted the Colcock child in New Orleans and the Judge Campbell portrait New Orleans; and the 3/4 length portrait of the reconstruction governor. He was associated with Fowler and V. Pierson. His painting of horses is second only to Troy, the celebrated American horse painter. The large canvas of the Metairie Race Track, which he did jointly with Pierson is an impressive assembly. It contains forty-four individual portraits. He established a studio at 51 Canal Street ca 1850-84, afterwards at 45 Baronne Street.

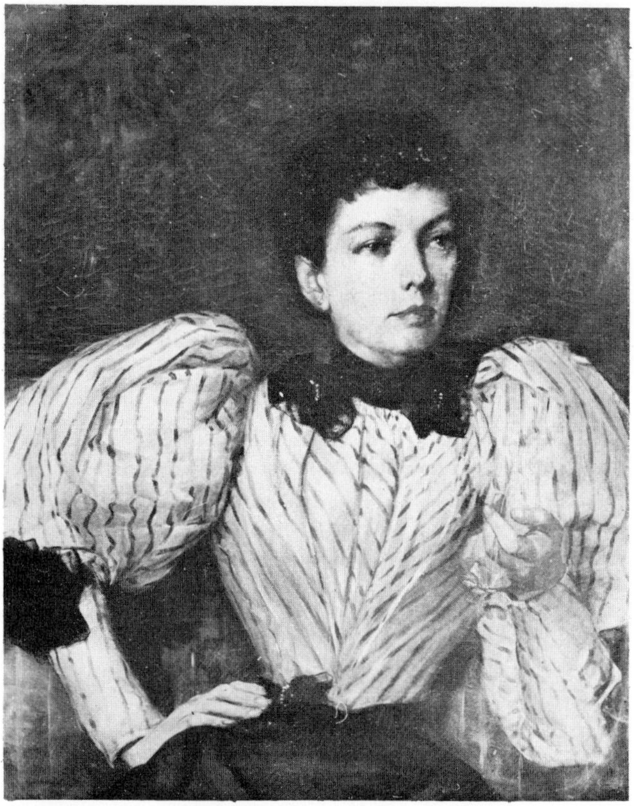

MORSE, EDWARD LIND
Young Creole woman
30" x 24"

signed E. L. Morse
1894

Morse, Esward Lind, 1857-1923

Painter of portraits and landscapes, son of Samuel Finley Breese Morse, student of Bougerau and Ferrier; a portrait of his father is in the National Gallery in Washington. Exhibited in the Paris Salon 1893, special exhibition National Academy of Design, exhibited extensively in the United States including the South. This portrait acquired in New Orleans could very well be a member of a local family. Morse successfully shook off the Barbizon tradition and produced a style of his own akin to Reid, Tissot, etc.

Molinary, Andres, 1847-1915

Born in Gibraltar, received training at the Academy of Seville and the Lucas Academy in Rome. Founder of the Art Union of New Orleans with Marshall Smith and Livingston; which was the first art school in New Orleans. The school opened in 1876. Painted many Supreme Court justices of Louisiana. His portrait of Achille Perelli (viz.) could not be better and his painting of birdshooting on the lake sums up the feeling of an early morning hunt.

"The portrait of an artist must show his life fiercely." Autobiography of Benvenuto Cellini.

"This morning all grey and still, set through with night mist, we flushed ducks; I shot from the boat." Friedrich Gerstaecker, Jagd und Streifzuege 1845.

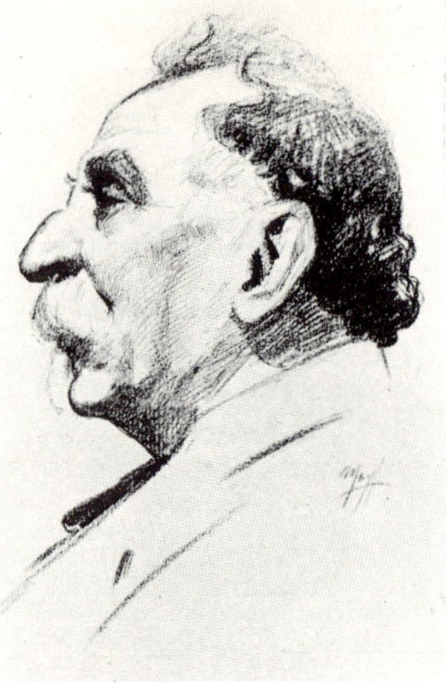

Pencil drawing of Molinary by Mayfield

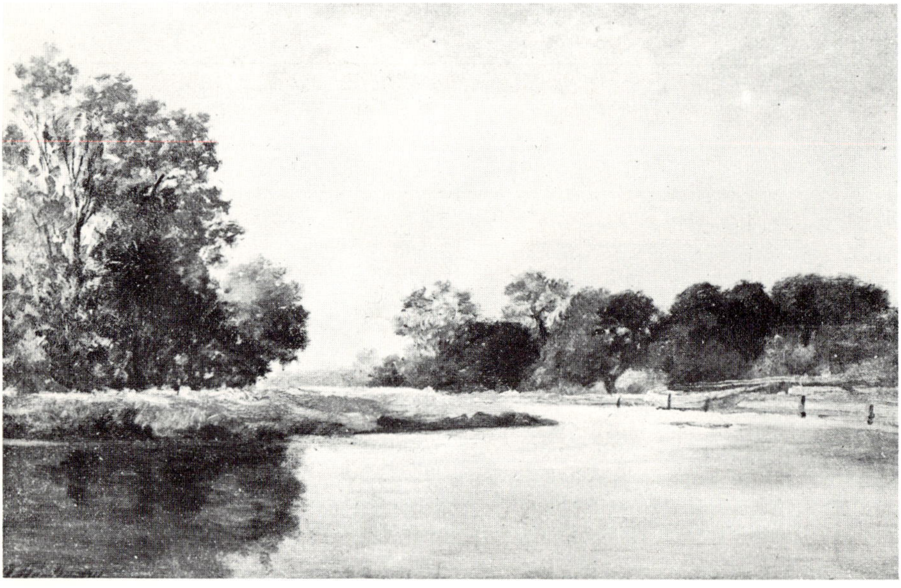

MOLINARY, A.
Pearl River
14½" x 21"

signed

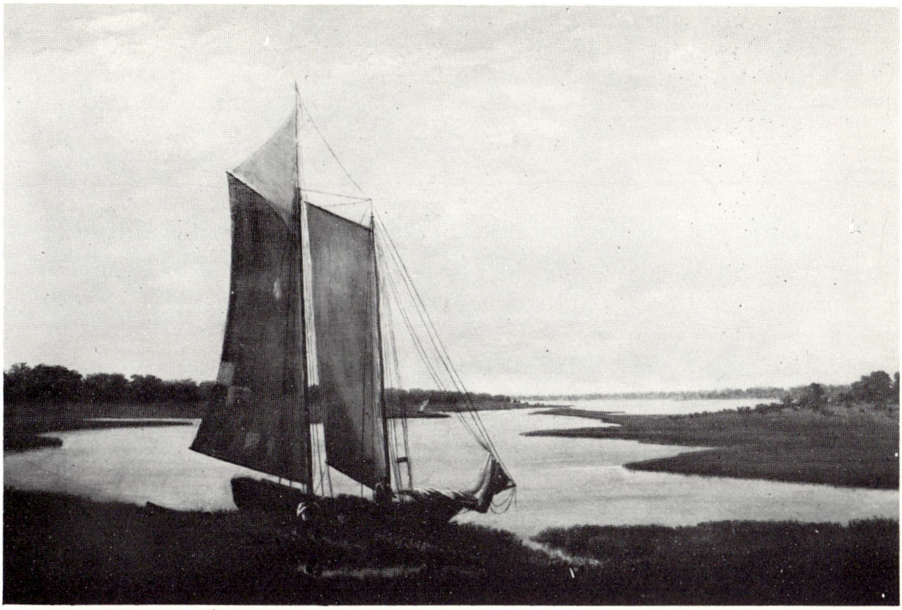

MOLINARY, A. signed ABM
Duck Hunting in the Louisiana Marshes
18" x 24"

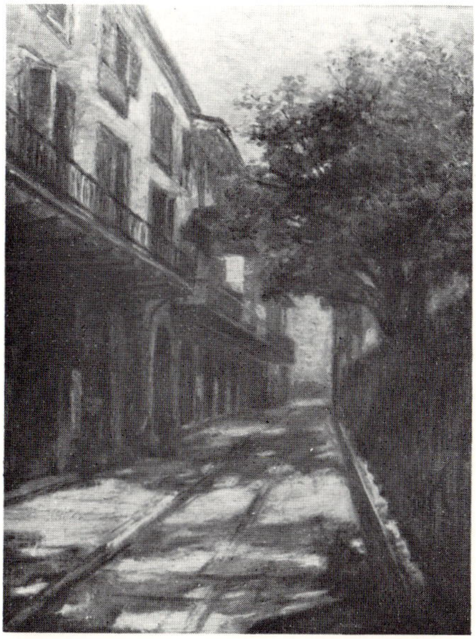

MOLINARY, A. signed
Pere Antoine's Alley
14" x 11"

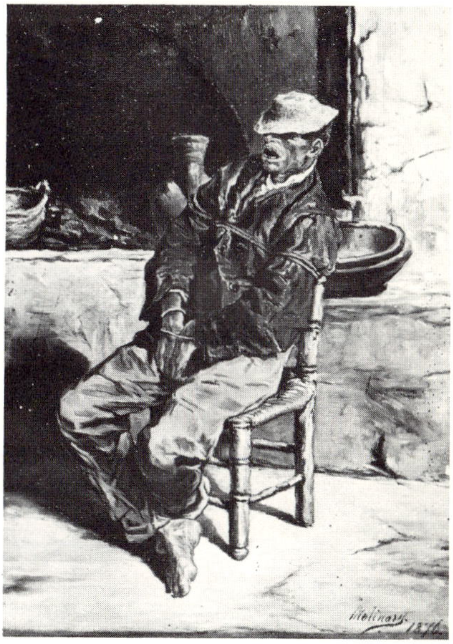

MOLINARY, A. signed: Molinary 1876
Prisoner
12" x 9"

Murphy, E. J., 1894

Nothing is known about this artist, except that there is a painting dated 1894, which seems to be of Lake Pontchartrain or Maurepas.

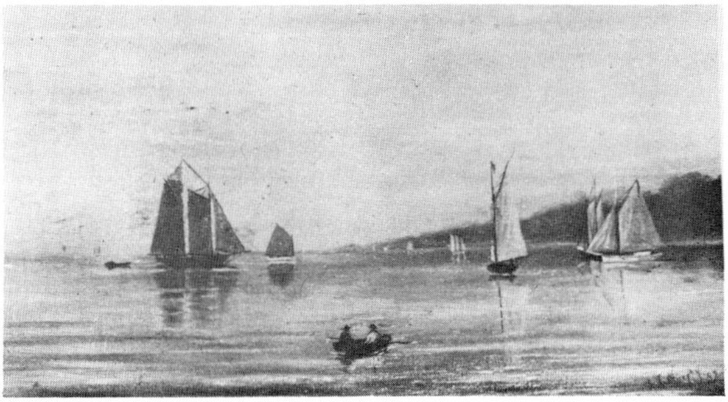

MURPHY, E. J.
View on Lake Pontchartrain or Maurepas
6½" x 12"

Signed E. J. Murphy
94

Neuser, L. A. W., 1837-1902

Born in Germany, came to this country with the 1848ters who were young people mainly dissatisfied with army induction and imbued with liberal ideas. We have a record of him in the newspaper "Creole" in 1856. As a capable portraitist, banner painter, and landscape painter, he settled in New Orleans until his death on September 30th, 1892. He is a completely professional painter and can be identified by the large green curtain partly veiling a generally yellow sunset, with a somewhat stylyzed bouquet in a footed glass. In all of the Neusers, especially in portraits, there is an emphasis on greens and yellows.

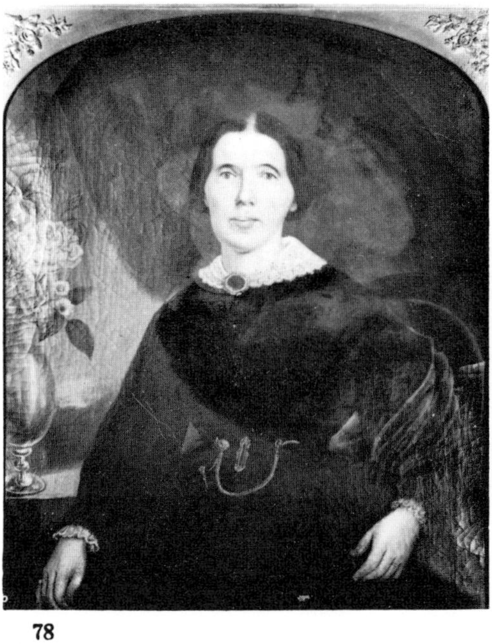

NEUSER, L. A. W.
Woman seated in Green upholstered Chair
36" x 29"

signed Wm. Neuser
1871

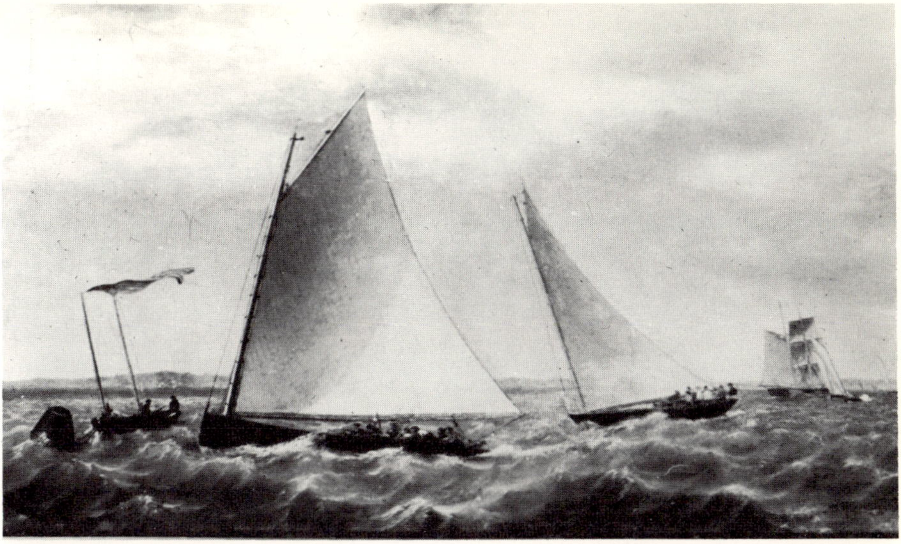

NORIERI, AUGUST
The Race
15" x 25"

Norieri, August, 1860-1898

This thirty-nine year young painter, produced some fifty paintings during his lifetime in New Orleans. If Samuel Clemens' "Life on the Mississippi" depicts and feels the soul of the Mississippi, then Norieri depicts the soul of the Mississippi steamboat. Not content with the hard and glossy delineation of the documentary painter, Norieri takes you on board and inside of his vessels, even though he only paints the outside. In the words of Kaguso of the Book of Tea "An object is not only the outside presented to the beholder but also the space that it contains".

The two cotton towboats in the collection have ladders attached to the stacks so that the pilot can see over the fog. The men and the fog are not painted but are there.

Horses glide like disembodied shadows and graze on a sandspit running into the gulf, with the protective promontory overseeing the scene. (the Sandspit) The same dreamlike romanticism is reflected in the jubilant rounding of the goal in the sail race.

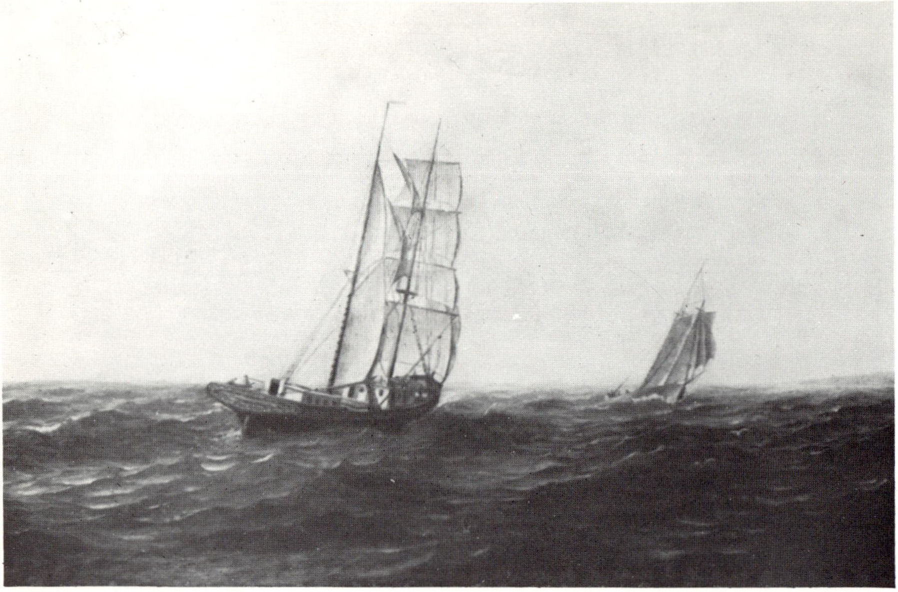

NORIERI, AUGUST
Two Fishing Boats
18" x 26"

signed Aug. Norieri
1889

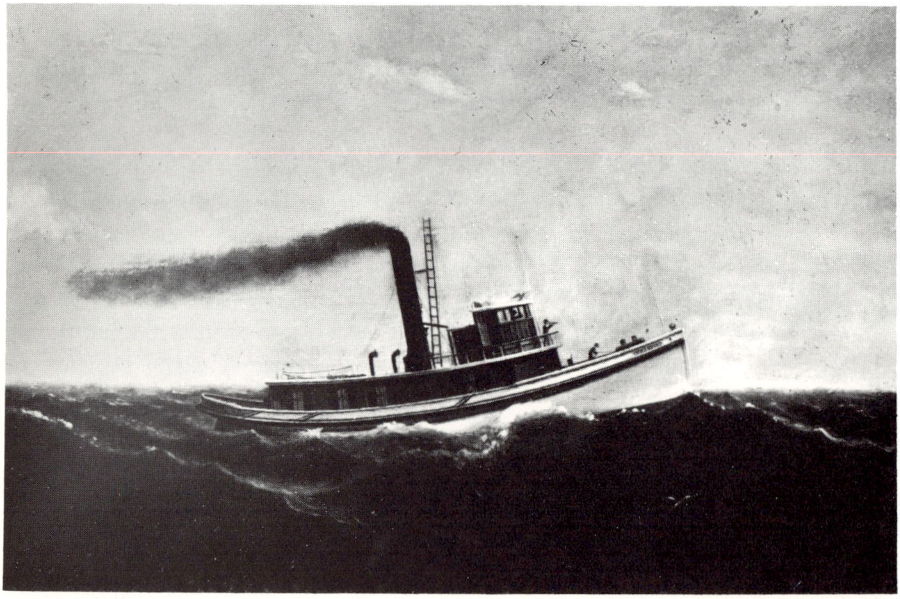

NORIERI, AUGUST
Towboat C. C. Keyser
22" x 30"

signed A. Norieri

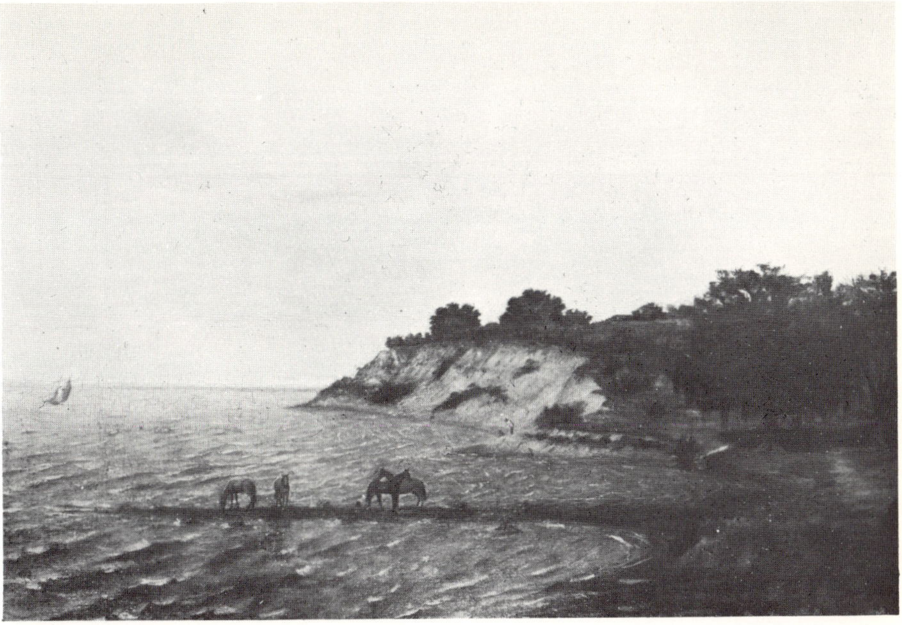

NORIERI, AUGUST
The Sandspit
26" x 36"

signed Aug. Norieri
1888

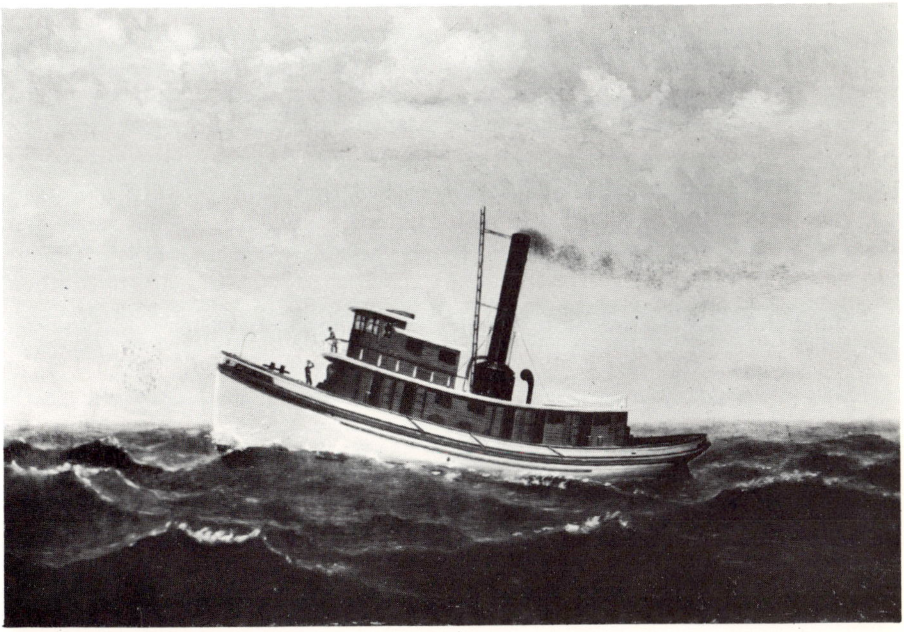

NORIERI, AUGUST
Towboat Joseph Cooper
22" x 30"

signed A. Norieri

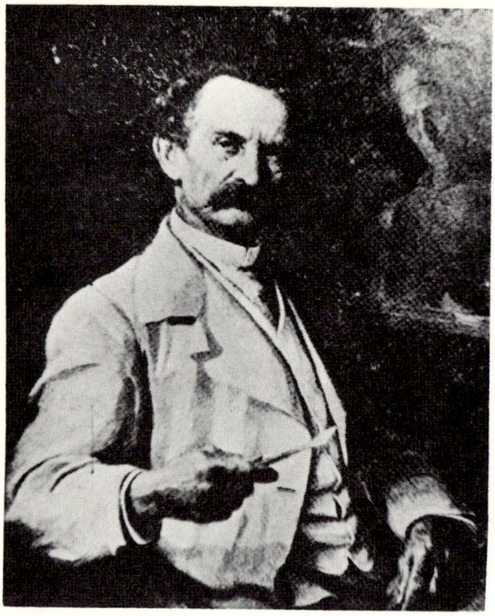

Portrait of Perelli
by MOLINARY
from a magazine cut

Perelli, Achille, 1829-1891

Born at Milan, Italy. Became a pupil of Antonio Galli, the Italian Thorwaldsen. Fought with the Garibaldi Freedom fighters for Italy 1848 to 60. We have a record of his studio at 464 Dumaine. He was extensively acquainted with the Molinary and Peretti circle. His birds, stillife and landscape, squirrels, deer, and shellfish are superbly painted. In this collection there is a pompano watercolor, which hangs from the characteristic square nail with the *trompe l'oeil* ribbon and a superb shadow, sublaying the ribbon.

The paint quality and concept rivals Audubon's renditions, and it may well be that the square nail stillife support device was originated by Perelli.

In the last year of his life he modelled the bronze bust of Dante, which is shown in the portrait by Molinary viz. It now surmounts the tomb of the Dante Lodge of the Masons at St. Louis cemetery #3. Another sculpture is a medallion over the tomb of the Army of Tennessee in Metairie Cemetery.

PERELLI, A.
Portrait drawing
signed: A Perelli
12¼" x 10½"

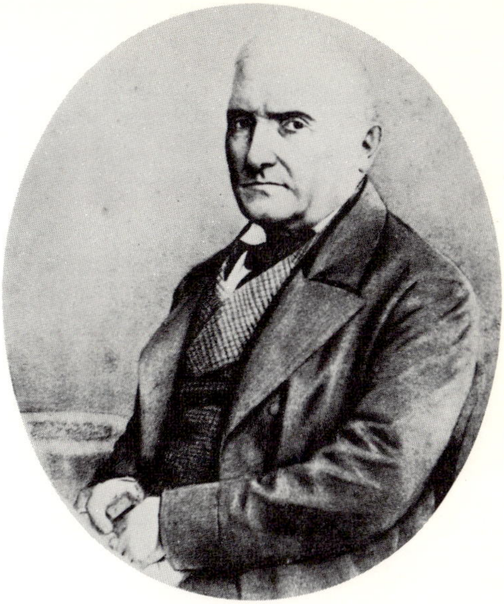

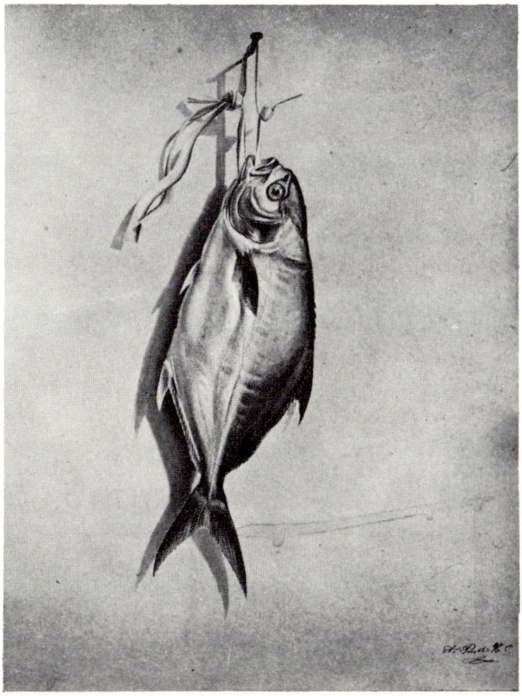

PERELLI, A., Pompano.
watercolor, 27" x 20½"
signed: "A. Perelli"

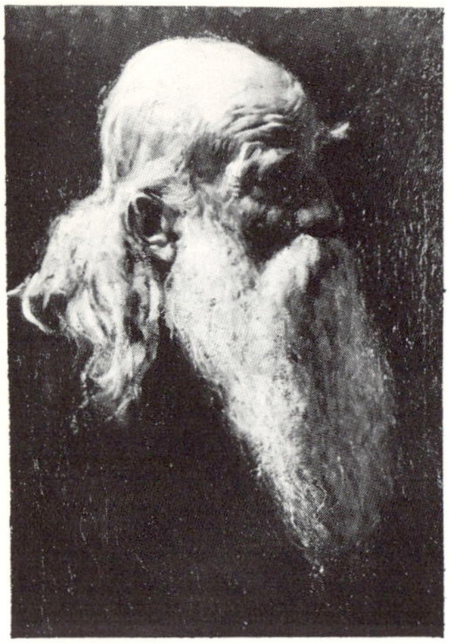

PERETTI, A. signed, '92
Head of Old Man
25" x 14"

Peretti, Achille, 1862-19 ?

Born in Allessandria, Piedmont, Italy, at twelve years of age, became self supporting, and exhibited at the various Italian exhibitions; won the Silver medal at Turino. He came to America in 1885 and was commissioned to do church frescoes; at St. Stephen's on Napoleon Ave., New Orleans and the church of St. Vincent de Paul on Dauphine Street, New Orleans. Sculpture also came easily to him. Several examples are known. Here is an academically trained artist, of professional quality, who carried on the Baroque tradition in the late 19th century. Tiepolo and Puvis, as well as Raphael, left their mark on him.

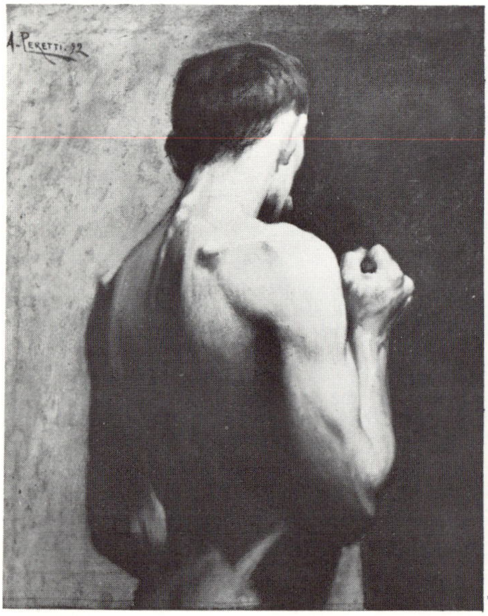

PERETTI, A. signed A. Peretti
Male Act (reputed to be J. L. Sullivan)
23" x 19"

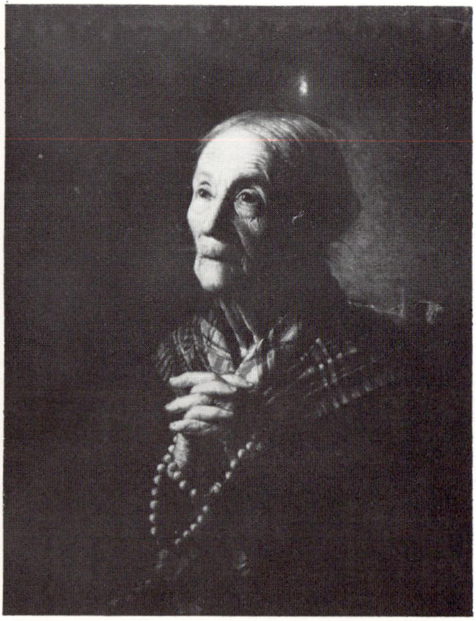

PERETTI, A. signed Peretti 97
The Prayer
34" x 25"

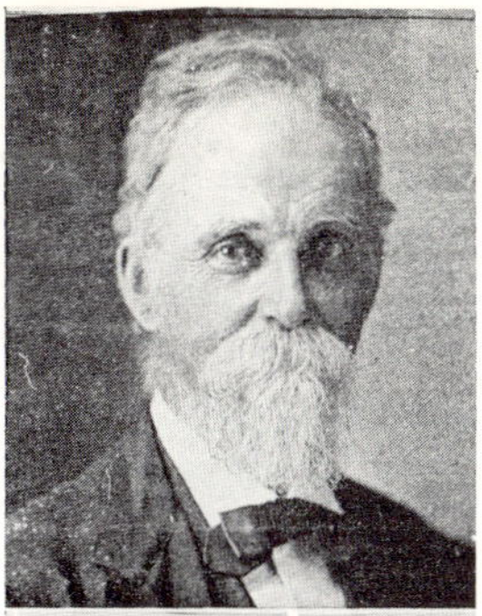

Paul Poincy,

Poincy, Paul, 1833-1909

Native painter, studied at the Beaux Arts in Paris with Gleyre and Cogniet. Enlished in the Confederate army and after returning became one of the founders of the New Orleans Artists' Association and taught in its school. Was for many years secretary and treasurer of the Association.

He was a finished portraitist and had a studio at 618 Commercial next door to B. A. Wickstrom. His "piece de resistance" is undoubtedly the large painting of the Fire Department at Canal Street, in which he collaborated with Moise in painting some fifty recognizable portraits. He was a superb painter of street views in New Orleans, one of these being our painting "Three-mule Cart on Decatur Street". The use of three mules dated from the passing of a city ordinance limiting loads for two mules to one ton.

POINCY, PAUL
Portrait of a Man
30" x 25"
signed; POINCY

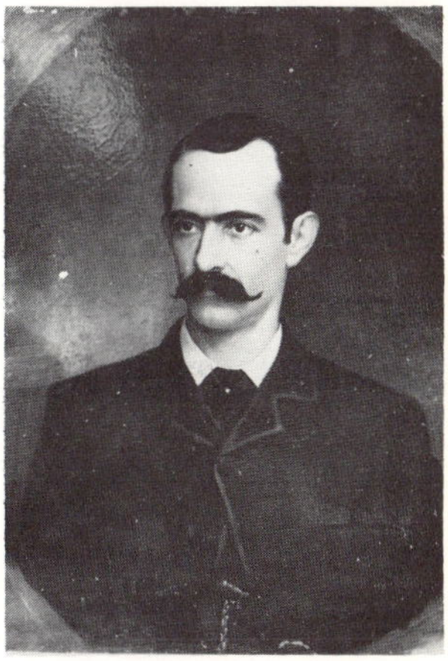

POINCY, PAUL
Three-mule Cart on Decatur St., N. O.
10" x 14"

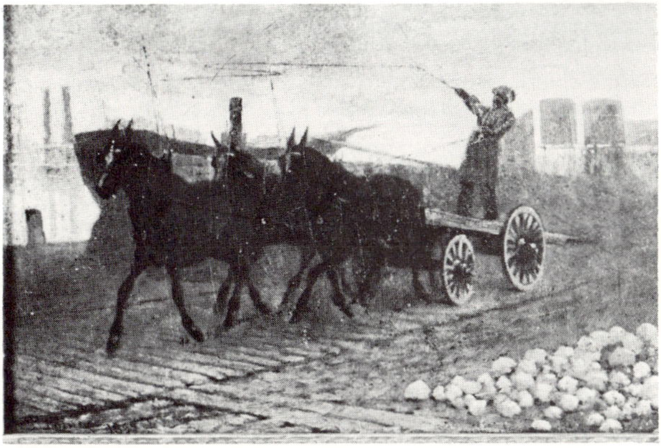

signed;
P. Poincy
1868

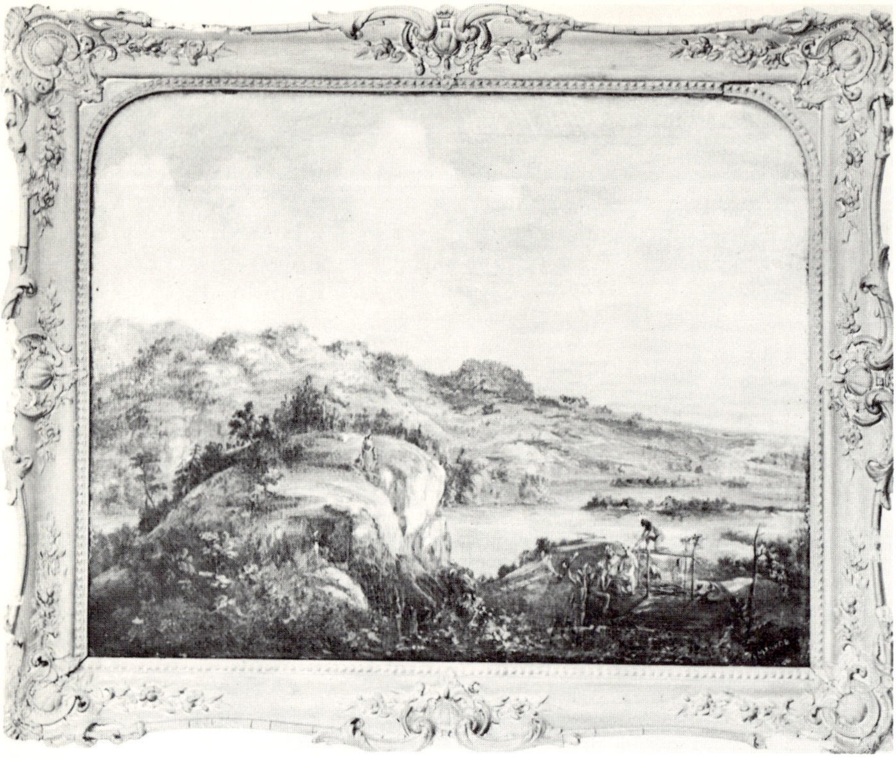

POMAREDE, Leon
Indian Burial

signed Pomarede

Pomarede, Leon, 1807-1892

Born in France at Tarbes, came to New Orleans in 1830. He married Clementine Mondelli between 1837-1840. He painted the decorations in St. Patricks on Camp Street, New Orleans. In 1843 he was again in St. Louis where he formulated his famous Mississippi panorama "From the Ohio River to St. Louis". It was perhaps 900 feet long, possibly painted in guache and possibly 12 feet high. It was presented on rollers and illuminated with gas lamps. The panorama is lost. It burned in Newark in 1850. The Panorama was shown in New Orleans in Armory Hall December 16th and January 3rd, 1849 and 50 respectively. Pomarede died from a scaffold fall sustained in Hannibal, Mo. The painting formerly in the Groves collection and now given to the University of Southwestern Louisiana, is most likely one of the smaller studies of the same subject in the Panorama.

Signed; Rinck, 1845

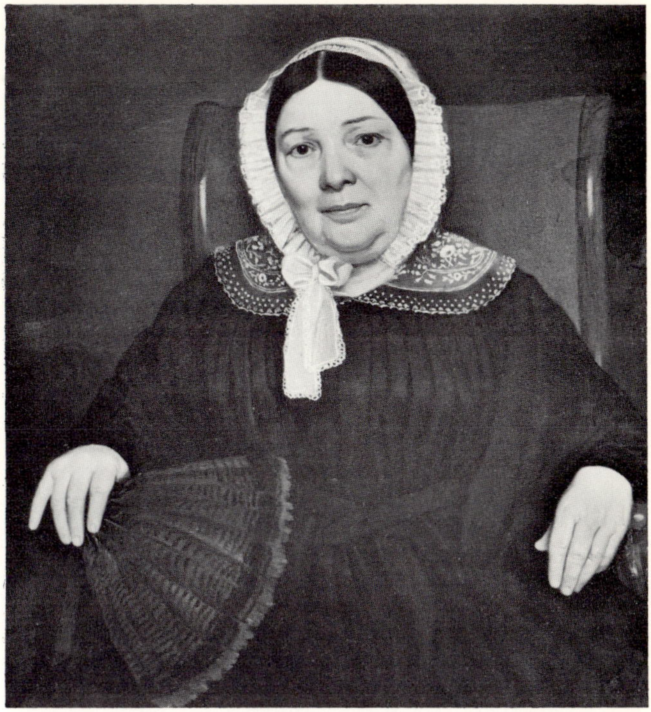

RINCK, A. D.
Portrait of a Creole Woman, 35½" x 28"
Courtesy Isaac Delgado Mus. of Art, N.O.
Gift of W. E. Groves

Rinck, Adolph D.

Studied at the Berlin Academy, in 1835 to 1840; he further studied in Paris. Painted the Mr. and Mrs. Franz Rust portraits from Reuter's "Stromtid", a popular German dialect novel originating in the 1830's. He came to New Orleans in 1840, and painted at Number 8 Pontalba Building off Jackson Square, in 1851. He continued until 1871, when we lose sight of him.

He was a professional painter of the socalled "Biedermeier" tradition, roughly analagous to the Ingres period in France. Sound training and subsequent technical proficiency is clearly apparent in his paintings. Beautifully grounded, well dried between stages, they never exhibit the reticulation and crackle that so many other portraits fell heir to in New Orleans. Vaudechamp's and some Amans' portraits and most of Buck's landscapes and some Perelli oils have the disease badly. Norieri and Clague, Feuille, Bernard and Boisseau, for instance, almost never flake or reticulate.

The Collection owns four Rinks not illustrated, two dated 1847, one 1861. The turkey feather fan is often found in the Rinck portraits of women.

Bibliography: Nagler KSTLRLX. vol 13 1843
Bellier Auvray Dict. Genr. vo 2 1885
Kat. Aust. Berlin 1836 p. 133
Benezit vol. 7 254.

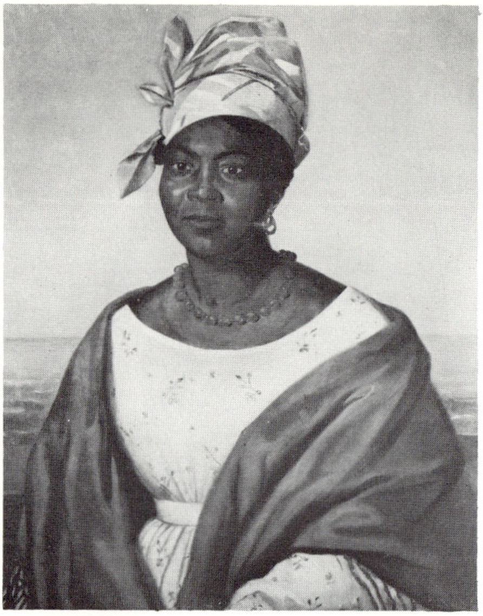

RINCK, A. D.; Woman in Tignon. signed; Rinck, 1844

Gift of W. E. Groves to the Univ. of S.W. Louisiana. The type of disfigurement of this portrait before restoration, especially the attempt to scratch out the eyes, indicated a fear of its power. For this reason, as well as the resemblance to another known portrait, makes it likely that this is a portrait of Marie Laveau, the famous Voodoo Queen. (Note: The wearing of the tignon was a requirement by city ordinance for "women of color".)
rf. I. M. Cline; Storms, Floods and Sunshine, illus. p. 112.

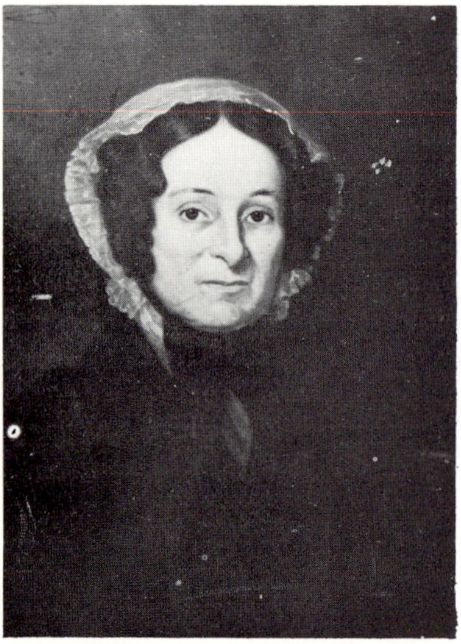

RINCK, A. D. Signed; Rinck, 1854
Female Portrait
30" x 25½"

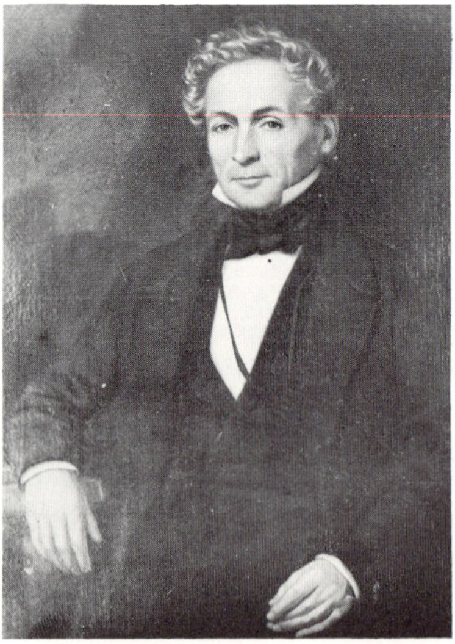

RINCK, A. D. Signed; Rinck, 1852
Male Portrait
38" x 30"

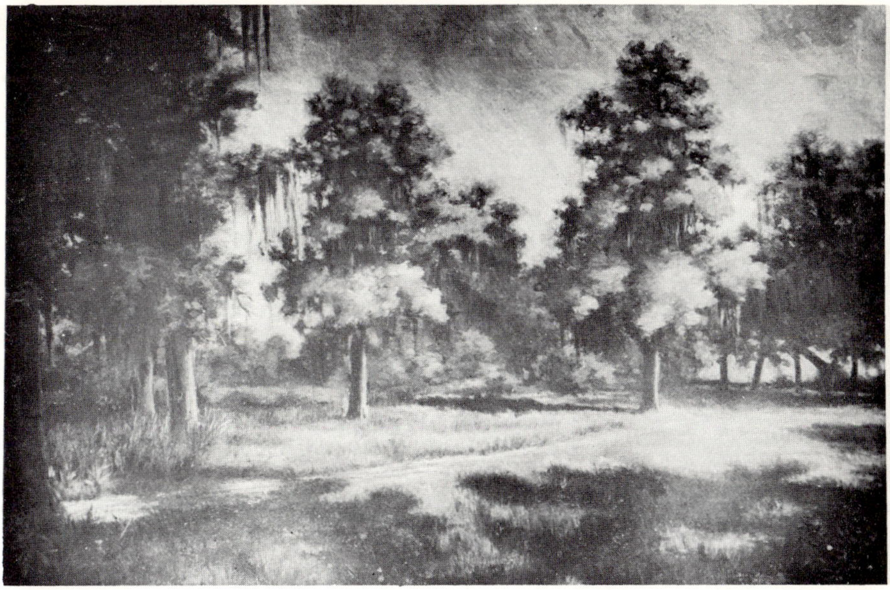

ROMANSKI, H.
Louisiana Landscape
30" x 40"

Signed; H. Romanski

Romanski, Harry, 1861-

Son of a well-to-do Polish family, came to New York after reverses in the family fortunes made it necessary for him to make his own living. Joined by his brother, an amateur artist, they set up a portrait studio, using the newly developed air brush, which soon fell into disrepute as a "mechanical device". Romanski then worked as an illustrator and for lithographic firms, and for several photo-engraving establishments, finally joining in a partnership in his own business.

By 1893 competition had become so great, he decided to emigrate to New Orleans where he worked briefly for two local photo-engravers, and was then taken on by the Daily States newspaper as Staff Artist. Subsequently, having already built up a reputation as an accomplished artist and writer, he again set up a photo-engraving company (The Romanski Photo-Engraving Co., Ltd.) serving as its President.

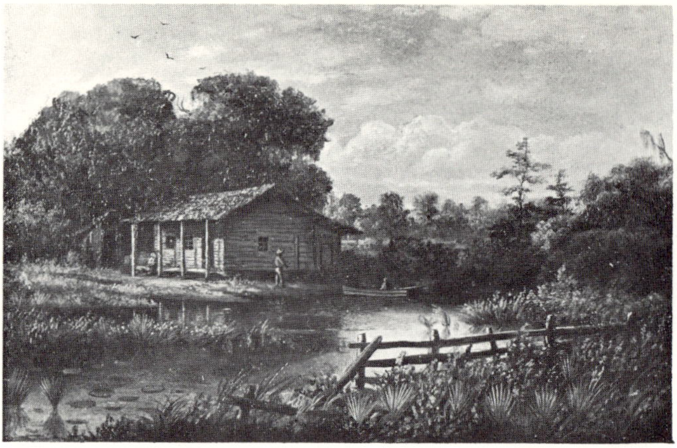

RUDOLPH, Harold
The Log Cabin, 14" x 20"

signed; Rudolph

Rudolph, Harold, 1850-1884

In 1871 had a studio at 212 Carondelet Street and in 1874 at 106 Canal Street. The Picayune in 1874 said that Rudolph was one of the best portrait painters. Brutus Ducomman, brother-in-law and partner of Rudolph, died in 1877. Rudolph had painted landscapes before this, as the Groves Collection has one dated 1876. Numerous seascapes have appeared, two of locations which seem to have Mexican conotations. There exists a very fine sunset painting of two men poling a boat under moss covered trees, of Clague like quality. Rudolph had a preoccupation with a "Walden" like environment, still quiet waters with gazing Indians, not aggressively standing but passively seated. The log cabin on the Bayou in its quiet isolation, could have served Thoreau and breathes a tone like the Bach choral, "I Have Lost the World".

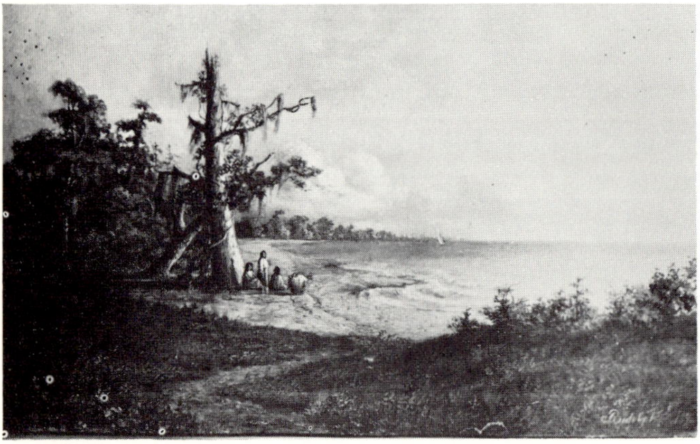

RUDOLPH, Harold
Indians on Lake
Pontchartrain
16¼" x 24¼"

signed;
Rudolph 1876

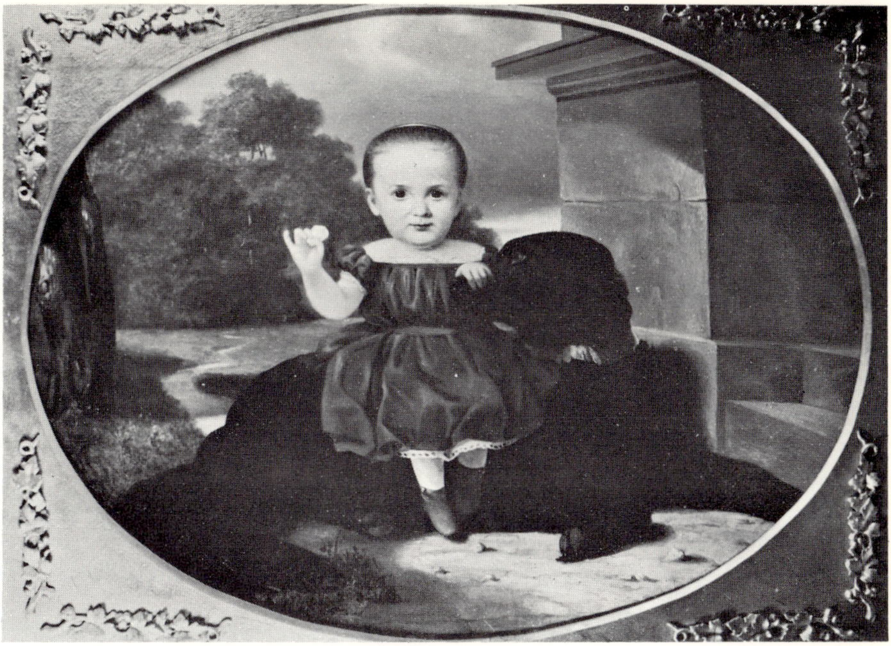

SEIFFERT, E.
Portrait of Child with Dog
33" x 44"

signed; E. Seiffert
1860

Seiffert, E.

An F. Seifert is placed in Mobile in 1859 who seems to be the same man. The E. in the signature on our painting is quite clear. The Mobile Seifert is also sometimes referred to with the double-f spelling. At any rate, this painting is a perfect example of the portraits completely finished except for the head which were taken around by itinerant portrait painters to be finished in one or two sittings, the purchaser choosing the type setting he preferred.

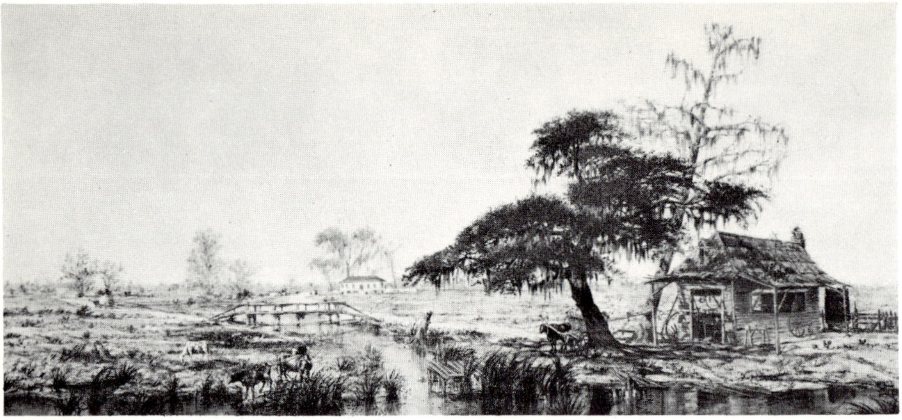

SMITH, J., JR. Signed; SJM
Bayou Farm, 17" x 36¼"
Courtesy Isaac Delgado Museum, N.O.; Gift of W. E. Groves

Smith, Marshall J., 1854-1923

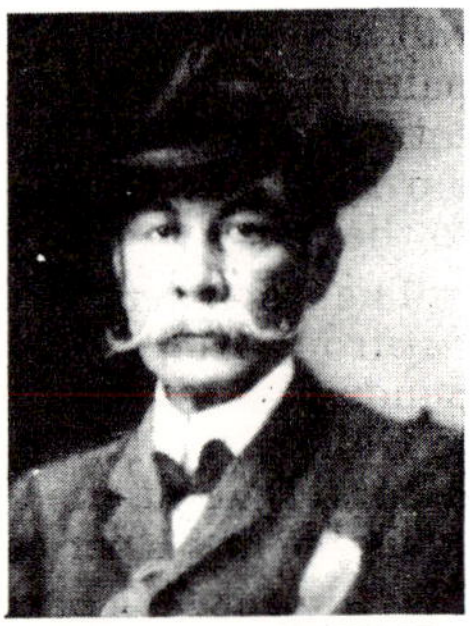

MARSHALL J. SMITH JR.

Born in Norfolk, Va., brought to New Orleans as an infant, refugeed in a Mississippi logcabin 1861 to 65, as the father was a colonel in the Louisiana volunteers. Studied art at a college in Virginia 1867, 68 and 69. Returned to study with Richard Clague, "the late lamented Creole who stands alone in his inimitable interpretations of Louisiana Scenery" (L.Q.C. in Artists of New Orleans, by May Mount, New Orleans 1896). After Clague's death in 1874, he studied with Theodore Sidney Moise and then went to Rome to study further. A painting of a Tomb on the Appian way, is in the Groves Collection. In 1876 he traveled to Munich, then housing the leading painting school, studied there, then went to see Gustave Dore in Paris, where he was presented with the Rossini etching by the master. In Atlanta, Ga., he opened a studio, and in 1877 married a Miss Belknap of New Orleans. He was one of the founders of the Southern Art Union in 1880, with Buck, Livingston and Molinary.

Marshall Smith was the logical outgrowth of the long tradition of Louisiana landscapists. His thorough grounding in Italy and Munich produced these superb, brown toned paintings. The Munich impasto, which is so strong with his contemporaries, and friends such as Frank Duveneck and William Chase, is very much in evidence in his paintings.

The language of the palette knife in combination with the brush, became a device in the late nineteenth and early twentieth century, with Remington, Goodwin, Sandzen and others in America.

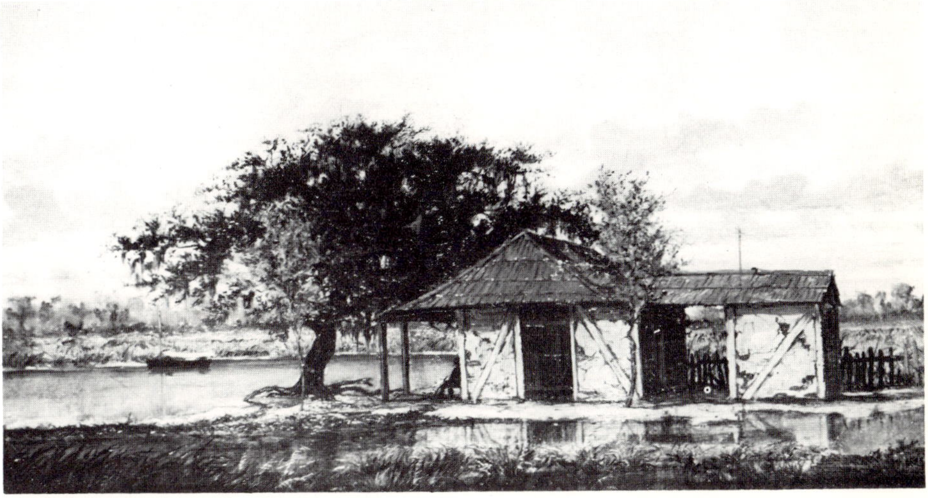

SMITH, M. J., JR.

Signed; M. J. S. Jr.

Home on the Bayou, 9" x 14½"
Note the breezeway and protected covered area for outdoor living.

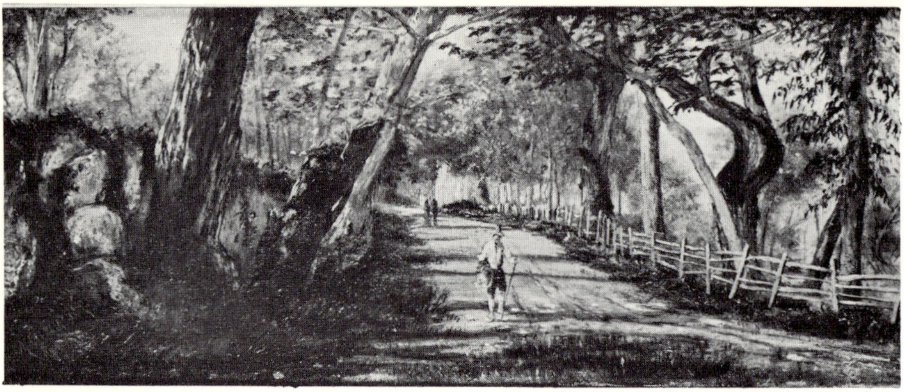

SMITH, MARSHALL J., JR.
Country Road
6¾" x 15¾"

signed; M. J. Smith Jr.

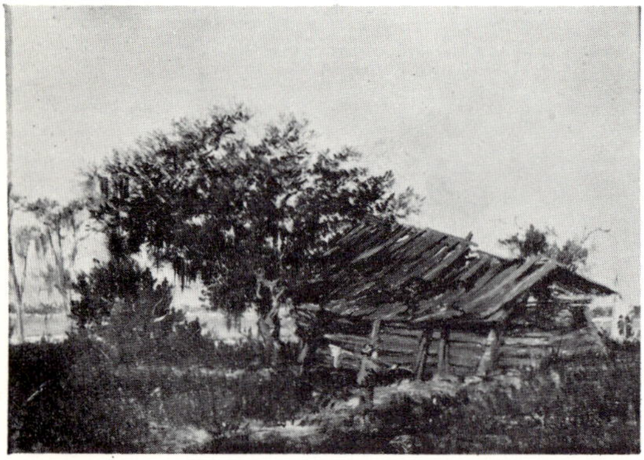

SMITH, M. J., JR.
Tumbledown Shed
6¼" x 8¼"

SMITH, M. J., JR.
Two Hunting Dogs
Signed; SMJ

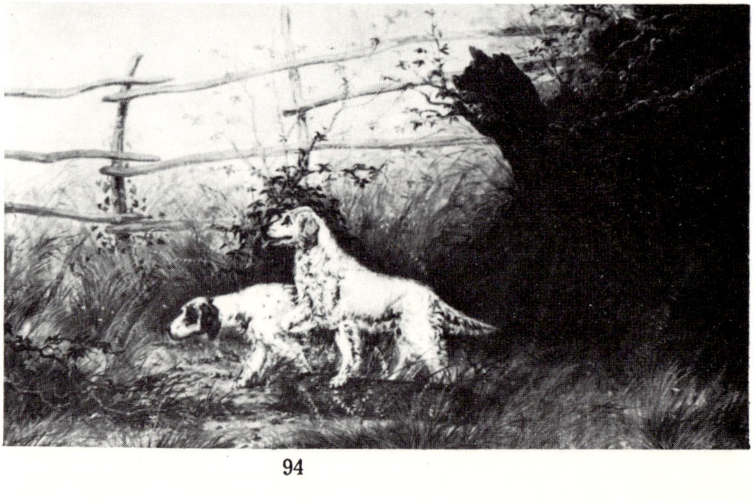

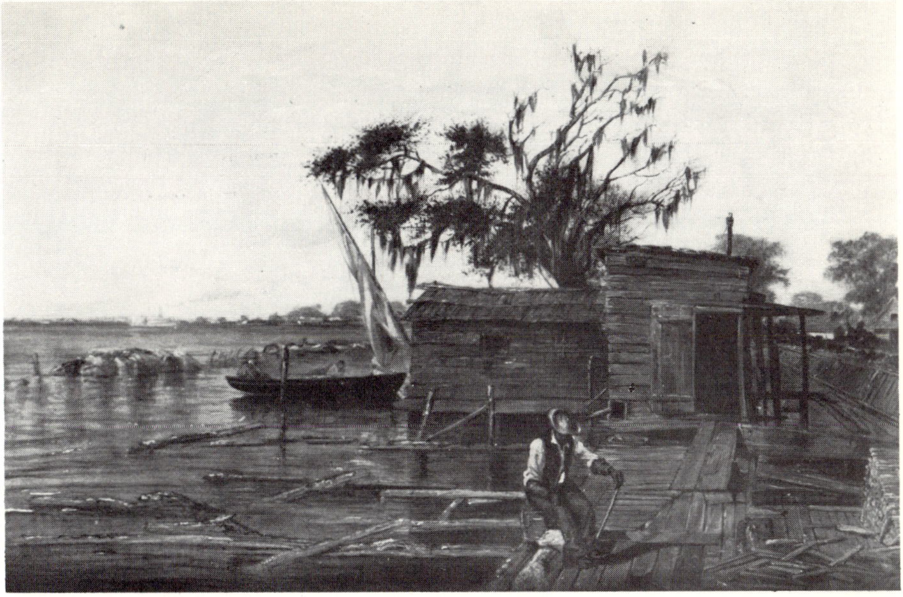

SMITH, MARSHALL J. (Signed)
Fishing Shack on the Mississippi.
Oil on canvas, 14" x 20"

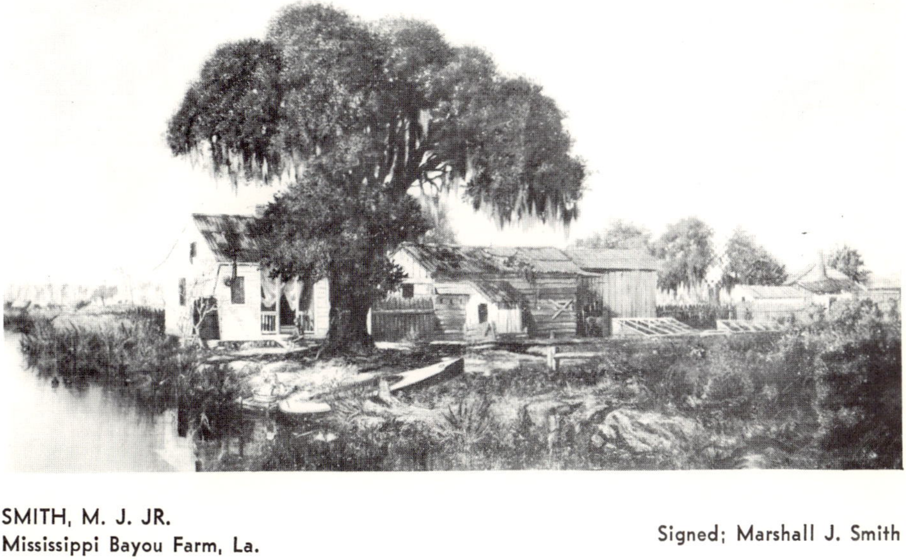

SMITH, M. J. JR.
Mississippi Bayou Farm, La.
15 x 26
Signed; Marshall J. Smith

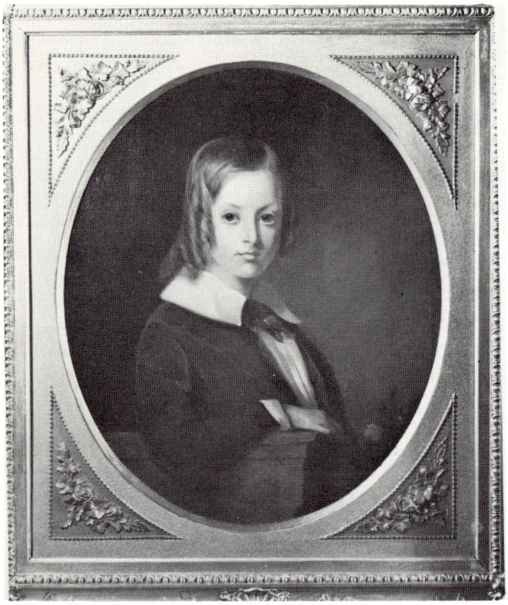

Sully, Thomas, 1783-1872

SULLY, THOMAS (attrib.)
Portrait of Master Collins, c. 1859
Courtesy Anglo-American Museum
Louisiana State University,
Baton Rouge, La.
oil on canvas, 29" x 24"

It has not been established that Sully was ever in New Orleans; it was thought so because he has been confused with the architect Thomas Sully, a nephew, who lived in New Orleans. However, there are a number of well authenticated paintings by him in the area. Presumably, as he was very much in demand as a portrait painter, those who could afford it went east to sit for him. The Sully influence permeated the South — Lambdin, Bush, Fraser, Jouett — all were affected, as were many eastern painters.

The Minor family has been prominent in Louisiana and Mississippi since the 18th century. The portrait believed to be Miss Minor came from the Chotard family into which she married.

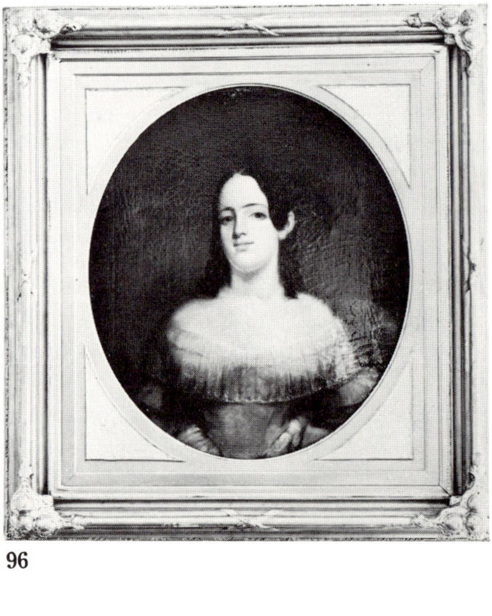

SULLY, THOMAS
Portrait of Miss Frances Minor, Natchez. The Sully register shows payment of $343 for portraits of "Misses F. & C. Minor" with frames and packing cases, 1816.
Courtesy Univ. of S. W. Louisiana
Gift of W. E. Groves

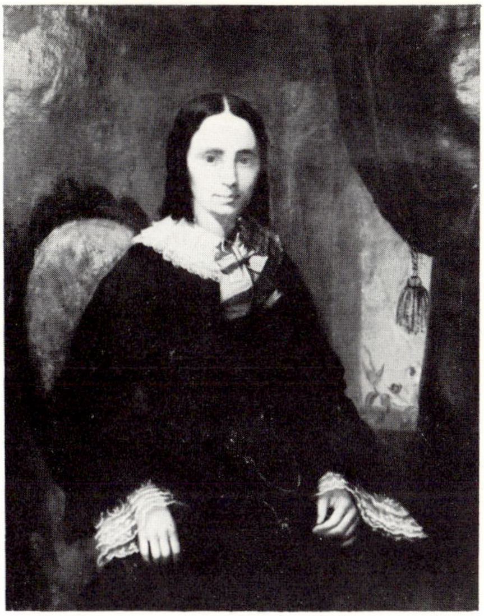

THORPE, T. B.
Portrait of Woman
42" x 34½"

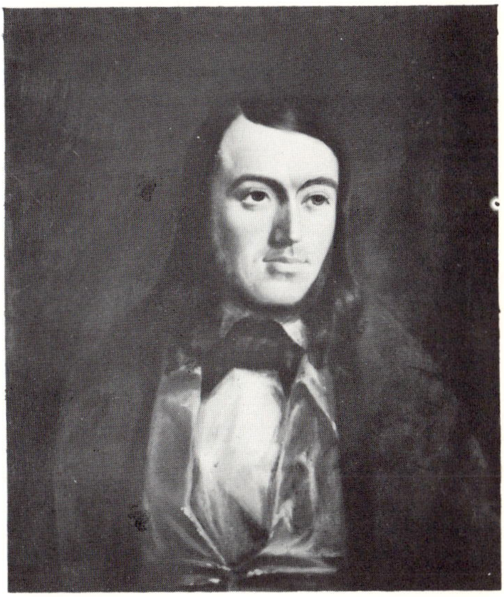

THORPE, T. B.
Portrait of Man in Red Vest
and Leather Jacket (attrib. to Thorpe)
42" x 34½"

Thorpe, Thomas Bangs, 1815-1878

Born in Massachusetts. In New York in 1830 lived with his widowed mother, and studied with John Quidor. After two years at Wesleyan University, he went South to visit, and returned in 1836 to spend 17 years in Louisiana. He was ambitious of creating great historical paintings, but 1836-39 found him painting portraits in Feliciana Parish with a studio in Jackson. In 1840 he moved to St. Francisville, and it is said he worked for a time on a newspaper in Baton Rouge.

The "Boy with Dog" shown here had Thorpe's name printed on the stretcher, and family tradition attaches the woman's portrait to his name. The handsome "Man in Red Vest and Leather Coat" ties in with the other two in style. The more primitive treatment of the boy is a characteristic often found in painters not experienced in painting children or animals, neither of which will sit still for long periods.

These three portraits should perhaps all be labelled "attributed", since a name printed on a stretcher is not necessarily inscribed by the artist himself, but the three seem to be by the same hand, if not Thorpe's, some unknown.

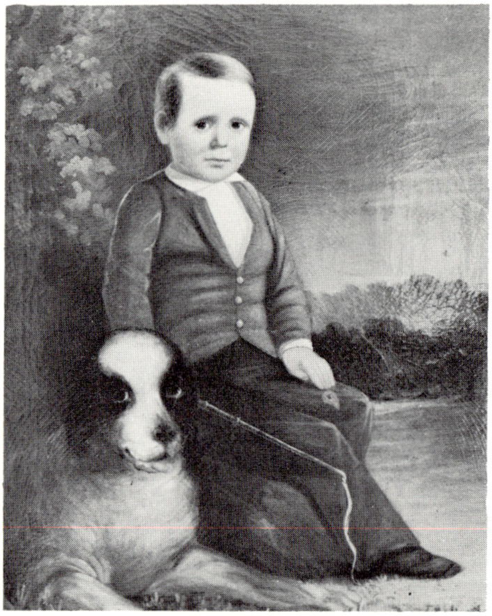

THORPE, T. B.
Portrait of Boy with Dog
Courtesy Univ. of S. W. La.,
Gift of W. E. Groves

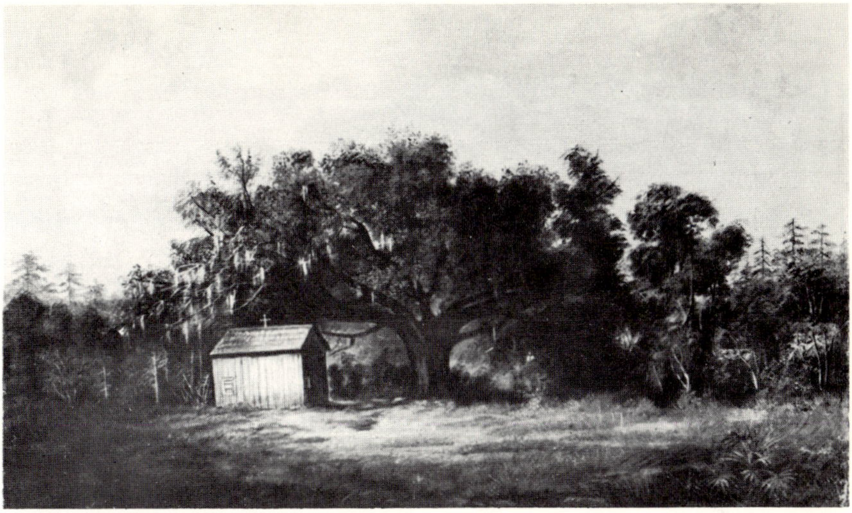

TOLEDANO, Albert
Country Church in La.
near Reserve
12" x 16"

signed A. Toledano

Toledano, Albert, 1860-1924

Self-taught painter, born on the Reserve Plantation, St. Johns Parish, La. Was apprenticed in Architecture in New Orleans to the architect James Freret. Was an auction plan painter, which means that he did the elevations and plot drawings for newly built houses to be sold at auction. A great many of these fine architectural color renderings exist. Along with these, he also did exquisitely detailed Louisiana landscapes, of which the collection has three. He also painted a number of birds of Louisiana.

Practiced architecture very successfully under the firm name of Toledano and Wogan.

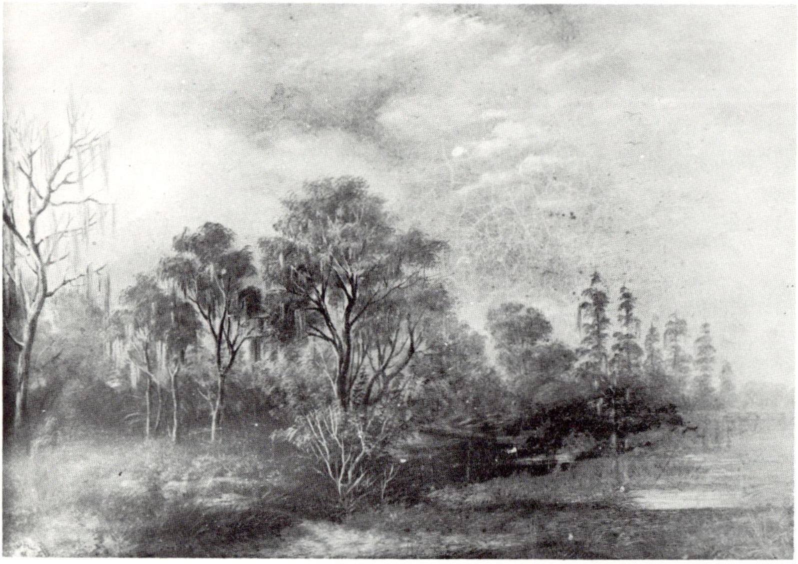

TOLEDANO, Albert
Louisiana Landscape
10" x 14"

signed A. Toledano

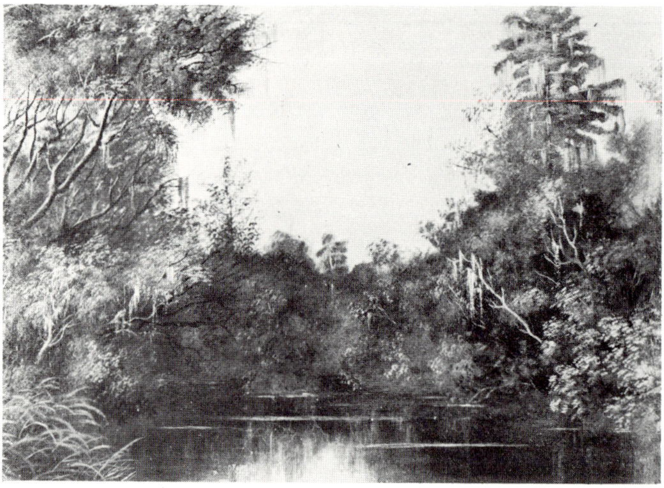

TOLEDANO, Albert
Louisiana Landscape
9¼" x 11½"

signed A. Toledano

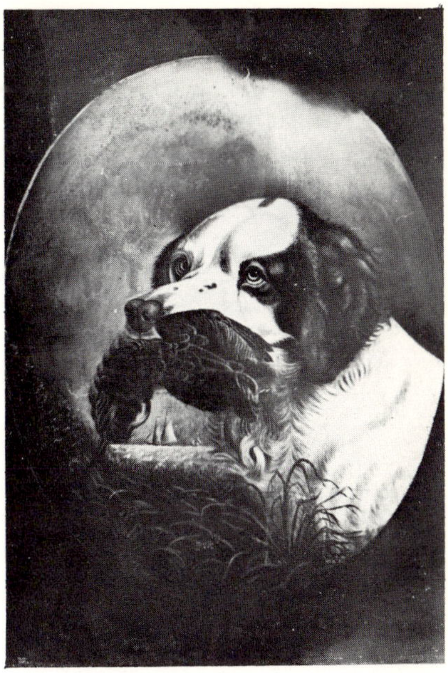

TUREAUD, F.
Dog retrieving Woodcock
Lake Pontchartrain in the
background, 27" x 22"
Signed, Tureaud, 1880

Tureaud, Miss F.

A member of the New Orleans Art Association, listed 1893.

Crawfish
by G. L. Viavant
see cover

Viavant, George L., 1872-1925

Represented by the delightful Crawfish on the cover of the catalogue, one of five watercolors by Viavant in the Collection. The "nature morte" subject matter was a heritage from his teacher, Achille Perelli. His other favorite subject was the swampy grass-surrounded bayous of the area where he lived. The Viavants were wealthy cotton brokers who lost their money in the Panic of 1897 and retreated to the country to "worthless property" not acceptable in payment of their debts. This property was 80 acres (originally their hunting preserve) located in East New Orleans at Gentilly and Downman Road, the site of the present Castle Manor real estate development.

Viavant supported his family by the sale of his watercolors of birds, the first of which was the cedar-waxwing, painted at the age of sixteen.

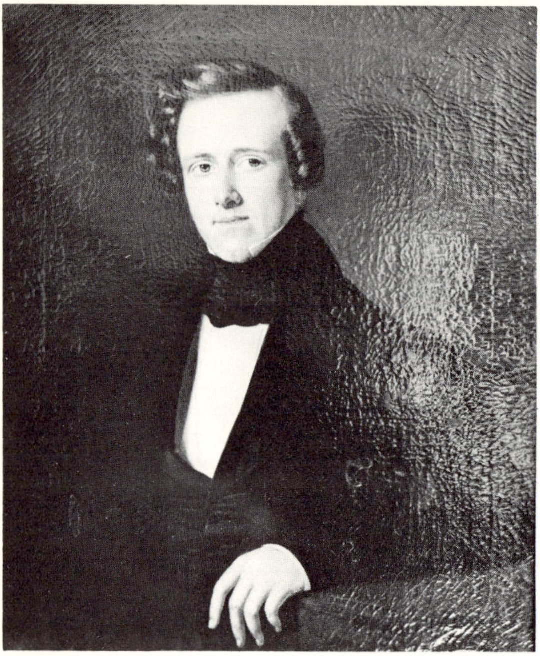

VAUDECHAMP, J. J.
Portrait, Courtesy of
Univ. of S. W. La.
Gift of W. E. Groves

Vaudechamp, Jean Joseph, 1790-1866

One of the best of the French portrait painters to come to New Orleans. In the winters of 1832-36 he recorded an astonishing number of members of well-to-do families of New Orleans, earning in three winters, according to Dunlap, some $30,000. His reputation was already established in France where he exhibited in the Salon from 1817 on. He is recorded as having a studio at 147 Royal Street, New Orleans, in 1833.

His paint is usually applied rather heavily, the occasional more thinly painted example surviving in better condition. He and others who came for short periods to Louisiana to do portraits must have painted on grounds hurriedly applied and improperly aged, as they usually come to the restorer with the crackled cupping shown in the University of Southwestern Louisiana example.

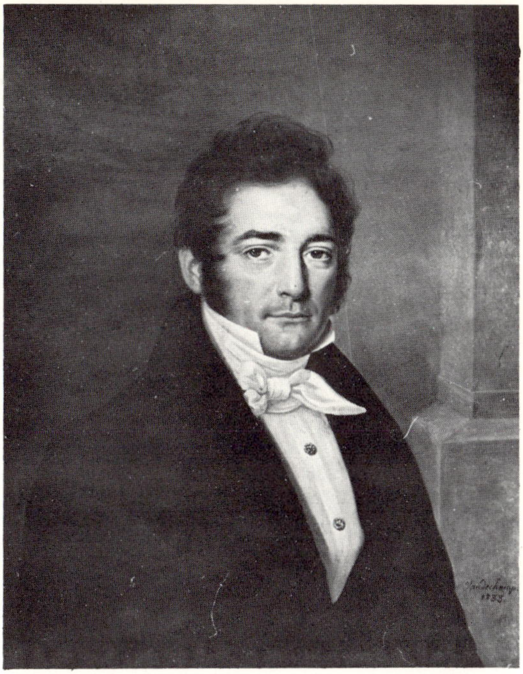

VAUDECHAMP, J. J.
Portrait of a member of the Ducros family, 32" x 25½"
Signed; Vaudechamp 1833

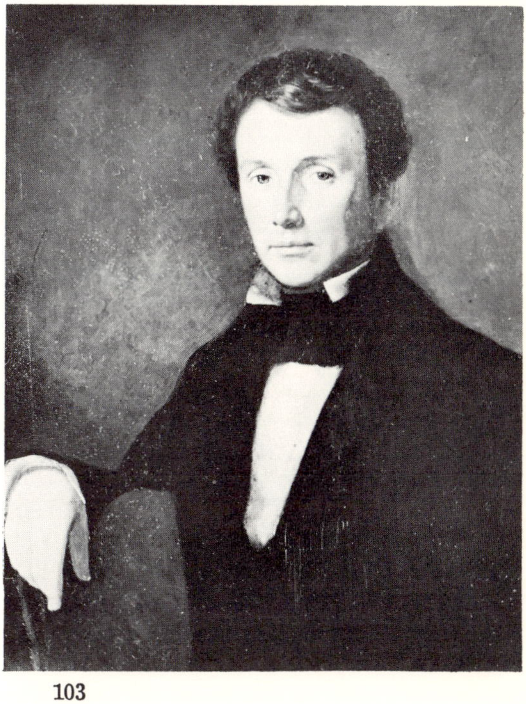

VAUDECHAMP, J. J.
Portrait of Man
32" x 26"

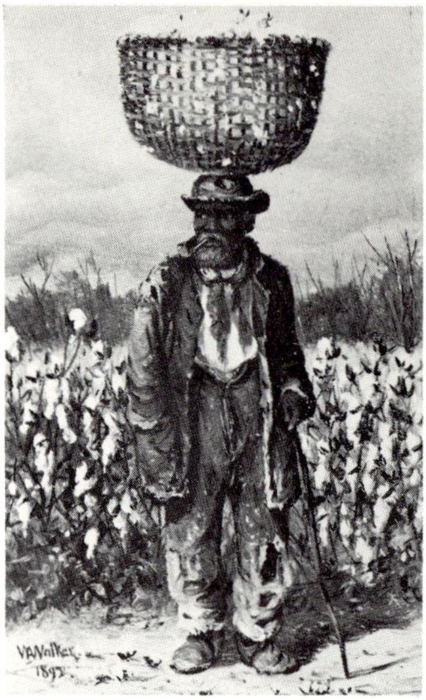

WALKER, W. A.
Cotton Picker
$7\frac{1}{2}$" x $4\frac{1}{2}$"
Signed;
WAWalker, 1892

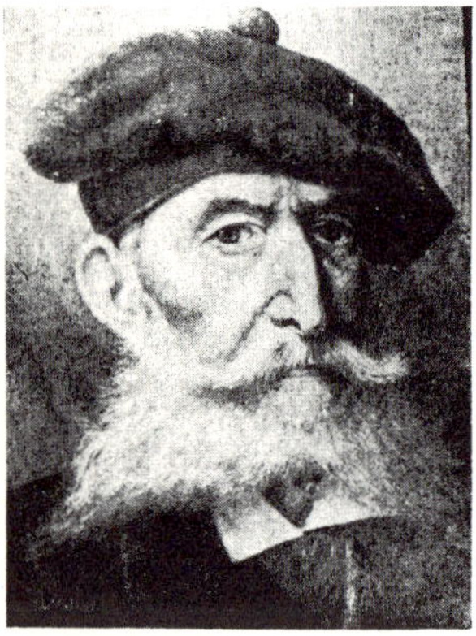

Self-portrait (from a newspaper cut)

Walker, William Aiken, 1838 (?) - 1921

A Charlestonian, exhibited in 1859 at the South Carolina Institute Fair as Master Walker. He worked in Louisiana in the eighties and is listed as active member in the Charter of the Artists Association of 1893. He was immortalized by the firm of Currier and Ives, "Printmakers to the American People", who produced two large folio lithographs in color from two of his paintings. One is the famous "The Levee New Orleans" dated 1884 and the other is "A Cotton Plantation on the Mississippi", 1883. He further exhibited fourteen watercolours and paintings in the first (1886) and the second (1887) exhibition of the New Orleans Artists Association. He was befriended by Mr. Gamble of Proctor and Gamble and spent his time there, making many fine topographical sketches on the Florida coast. These sketches could be a basis for a navigational Atlas or Pilotbook, and are in every respect equal to the drawings in the famous Atlantic Neptune of the 18th century, which were the Atlases used by the British Admiralty in respect to the American Coast.

Walker was aided in his small sketches of black country people by the camera, with which he took notes. His character sketches did not have the quality of a Julio or Homer, but make up in spirit what they lack in technique. His cabin scenes, external views only, have a totally at home quality and exude an empathy that is unequalled in American painting; not even the Eastman Johnson, Mount and Bingham Genre pieces have achieved this sweet simplicity.

A musician also, he possessed the social graces to a degree that enabled him to charm everyone he met. He died in Charleston, South Carolina.

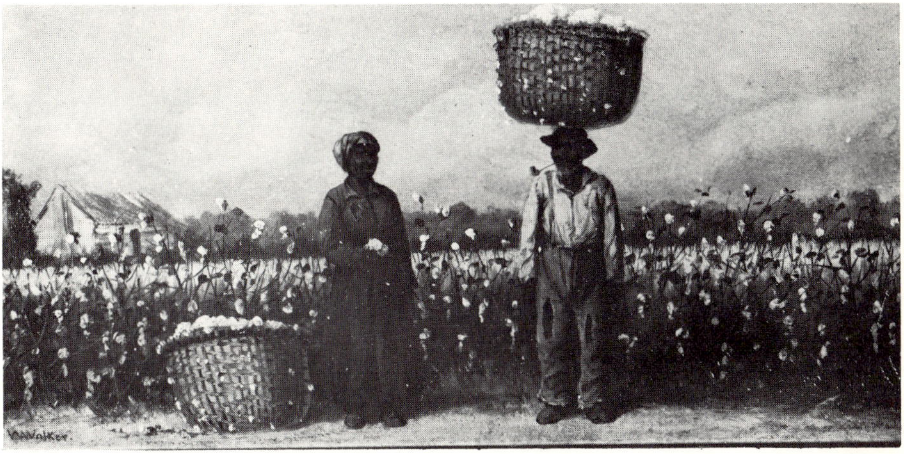

WALKER, W. A.
Negroes in Cotton Field
6 1/8" x 12 1/2"

Signed; WAWalker

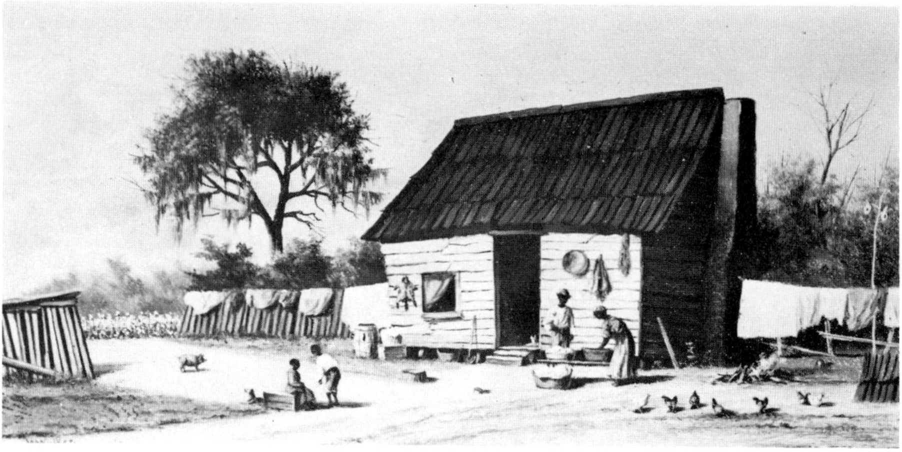

WALKER, W. A.
Wash Day; 6¾" x 12¾"

Signed; WAWalker

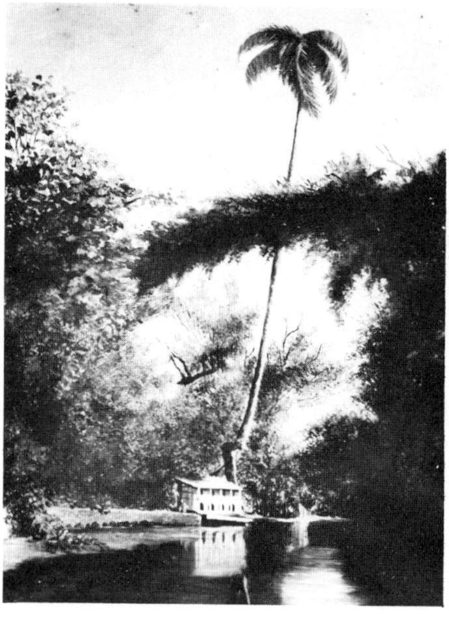

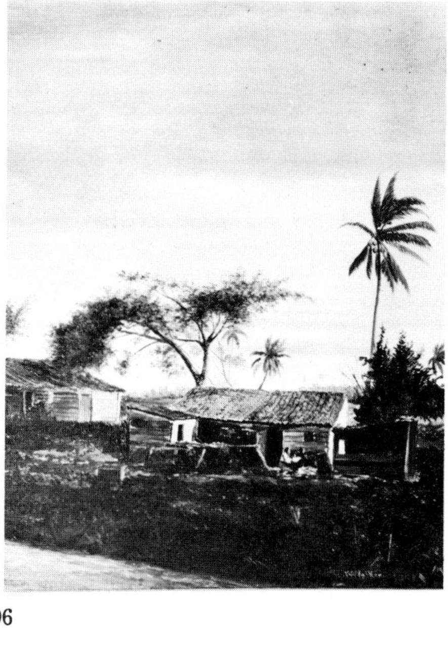

WALKER, W. A.
Two Scenes in Florida (or Cuba)

Signed;
WAWalker

Wikstrom, Bror Anders, 1854-1909

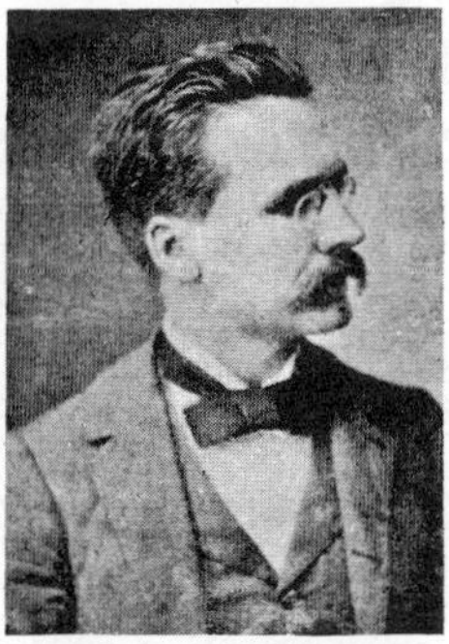

BROR A. WIKSTROM

Born in Sweden, had studied in Europe before coming to New Orleans in 1883. Four years later he launched a periodical called Art and Letters which lasted for only a short run in spite of his enlistment of the gifted writers of the area. Became a leading designer of New Orleans carnival pageantry which augmented his income so that he could live comfortably and travel to Europe frequently.

He joined with Molinary, Poincy, Marshall Smith and others in the formation of the Southern Art Union, offering the first art training available to local students. His studio was for many years on the top floor of a building in Commercial Place, which also housed the studio of Paul Poincy. He painted a variety of subjects, but is best known for his fine marines.

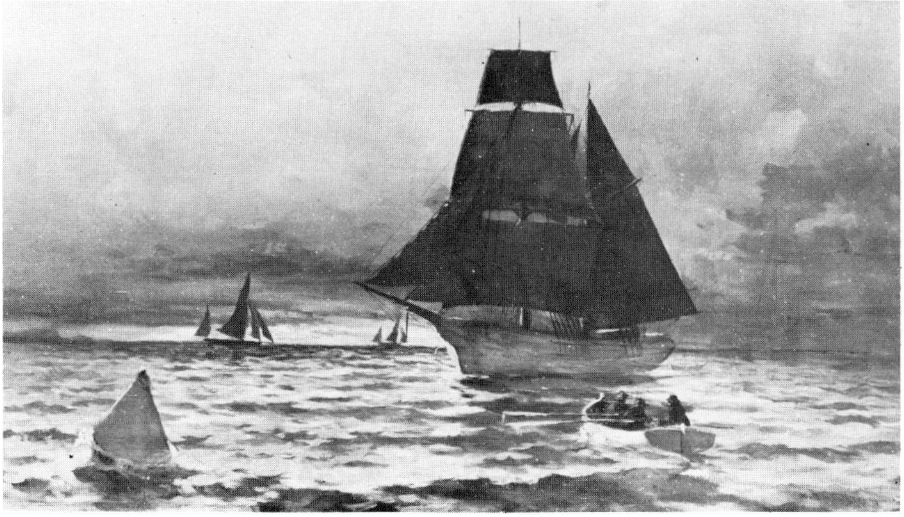

WIKSTROM, B. A.
Marine Painting
17" x 30"

Signed; B. A. Wikstrom

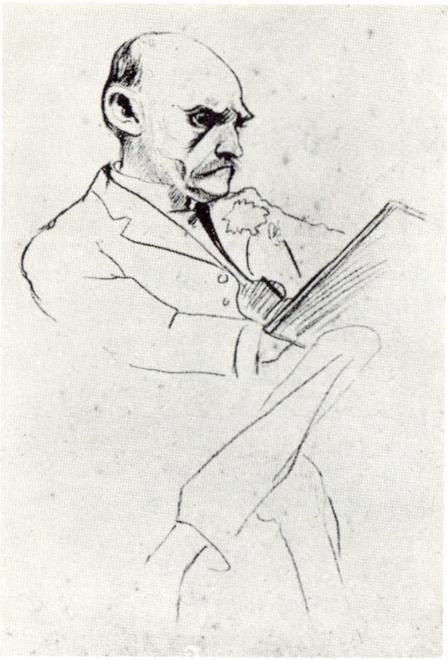

Caricature of Woodward
drawn in the Sketch Club
by MAYFIELD

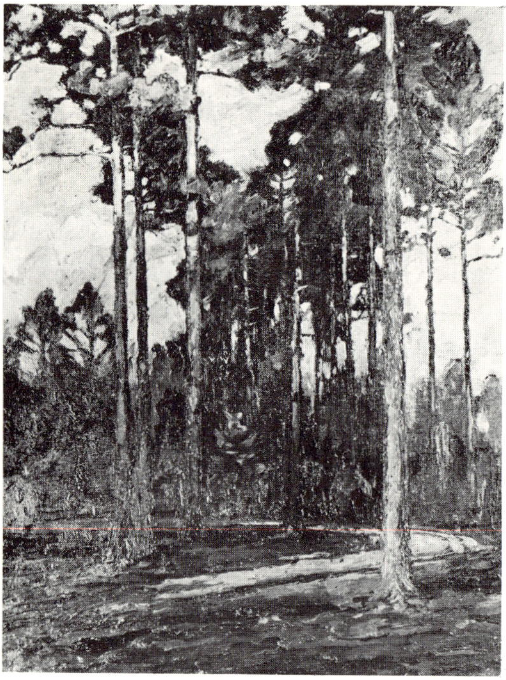

WOODWARD, ELLSWORTH
Southern Pines
24" x 18"

Woodward, Ellsworth, 1861-1939

Born in Massachusetts, studied at the Rhode Island School of Design, and at Munich. Was for many years director of the School of Art at Newcomb College, Tulane University, New Orleans. His brother, William, was also a gifted artist and teacher of drawing at Tulane and Newcomb. Both were among those recorded in Mayfield's sketches done at gatherings of the "Sketch Club", and both were at various times officers of the Art Association.

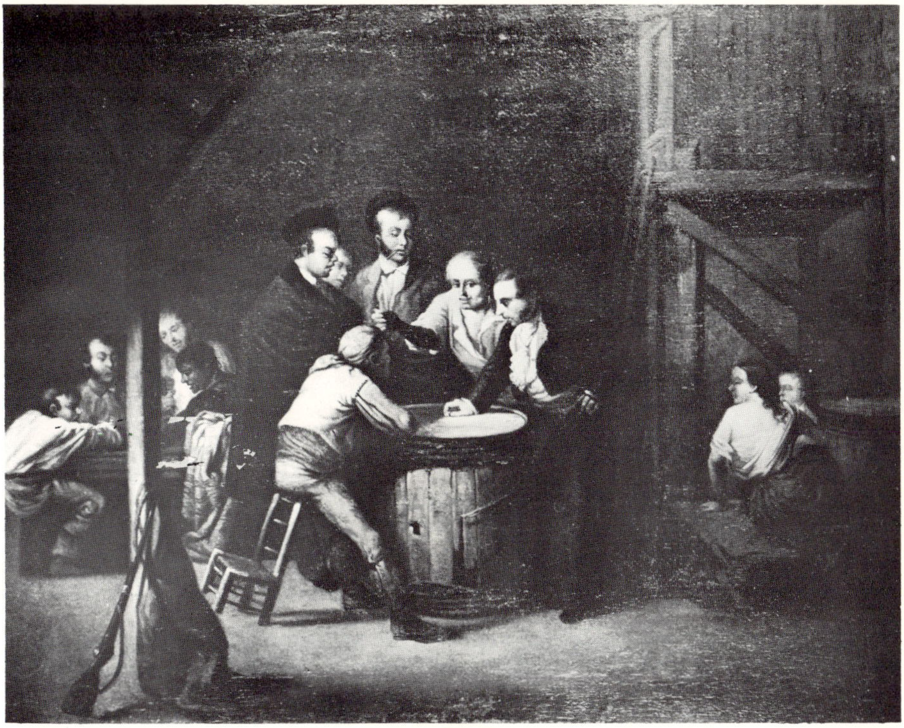

C(?). M. FORTEZA
Gambling Scene
35½" x 25"

Signed?

An Enigma

Whether this painting belongs with the Louisiana scene is an as yet unsolved puzzle. The subject suggests a meeting of Jean Lafitte and his friends although it could be in a quite different locale. What seems to be a signature (?), C. M. FORTEZA, is inscribed on a box, trunk, or pile of blankets on which the woman with the child sits. No artist of this name is known who could be remotely connected with New Orleans. The red sashed bluecoated figure is holding a die and looks French, the two standing figures look Spanish, there is an Indian with a blanket and some other questionable characters sitting to the left. It seems made to order for an illustration of Lafitte gambling for high stakes. A fine conversation piece resembling a Mount interior or one of Eastman Johnson's barn assemblies. A further parallel would be Thomas W. Wood, Bingham or Beard.

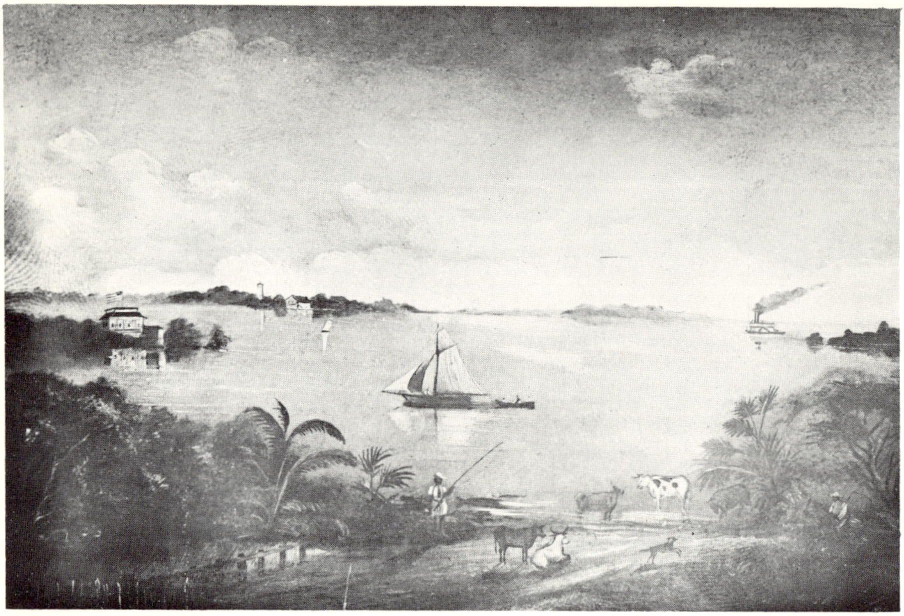

UNKNOWN PAINTER
Balize
17" x 24½"

Ocean vessels were guided up the river by pilots who lived with their families and the families of fishermen at a settlement called Balize near the mouth of the river. At this spot was a wooden lighthouse designed by Benjamin Latrobe, superceded later by a masonry one. All remnants of this lonely outpost have long since disappeared.

Quotations from: "Nach Amerika" by Friedrich Gerstaeker,
Jena, 1855

The Captain of the sidewheeler stood over the wheel-housing with a megaphone, "Where do you hail from?" We could hear the noise of the wheels as the towboat approached us. We reefed our sails and the heat was wet and depressing. There was not a breath of air; neither hill nor cottage was visible; a flat and lonely coast strip appeared in the distance. Finally the steamboat took us in tow. Very slowly we proceeded against the strong current and we saw some buildings appearing on either the right or the left as we followed the river's turns. We finally arrived at a place where a number of wooden buildings on posts were erected in a terrible swamp. They were connected with slender planks. This so-called Balize was a sad sight; one could not imagine that people could exist under these conditions.

Quotation from: Domestic Manners of the Americans

by Mrs. Trollope 1832

The first indication of our approach to land was the appearance of this mighty river pouring forth its muddy waters, and mingling with the deep blue of the Mexican Gulf. The shores of this river are so utterly flat, that no object is perceptible at sea . . . Large flights of pelicans were seen standing upon the long masses of mud which rose above the surface of the waters, and a pilot came to guide us over the bar, long before any other indication of land was visible.

I never beheld a scene so utterly desolate as this entrance of the Mississippi. Had Dante seen it, he might have drawn images of another Bolgia from its horrors. One only object rears itself above the eddying waters; this is the mast of a vessel long since wrecked in attempting to cross the bar —

By degrees bulrushes of enormous growth become visible, and a few more miles brought us within sight of a cluster of huts called the Balize, by far the most miserable station that I ever saw made the dwelling of man; but I was told that many families of pilots and fishermen lived there.

For several miles above its mouth, the Mississippi presents no objects more interesting than mudbanks, monstrous bulrushes and now and then a huge crocodile luxuriating in the slime. Another circumstance that gives this dreary scene an aspect of desolation, is the incessant appearance of vast quantities of driftwood, which is ever finding its way to the different mouths of the Mississippi. Trees of enormous length, sometimes still bearing their branches, and still oftener their uptorn roots entire, the victims of the frequent hurricane, come floating down the stream. Sometimes several of these, entangled together, collect among their boughs a quantity of floating rubbish, that gives the mass the appearance of a moving island bearing a forest . . . this, as it approaches . . . looks like the fragment of a world in ruins. The banks continue invariably flat, but a succession of planless villas . . . sometimes surrounded by their sugar grounds and negro huts, varied the scene . . . For a length of one hundred and twenty miles from the Balize to New Orleans, and one hundred miles above the town, the land is defended from the encroachment of the river by a high embankment called the levee.

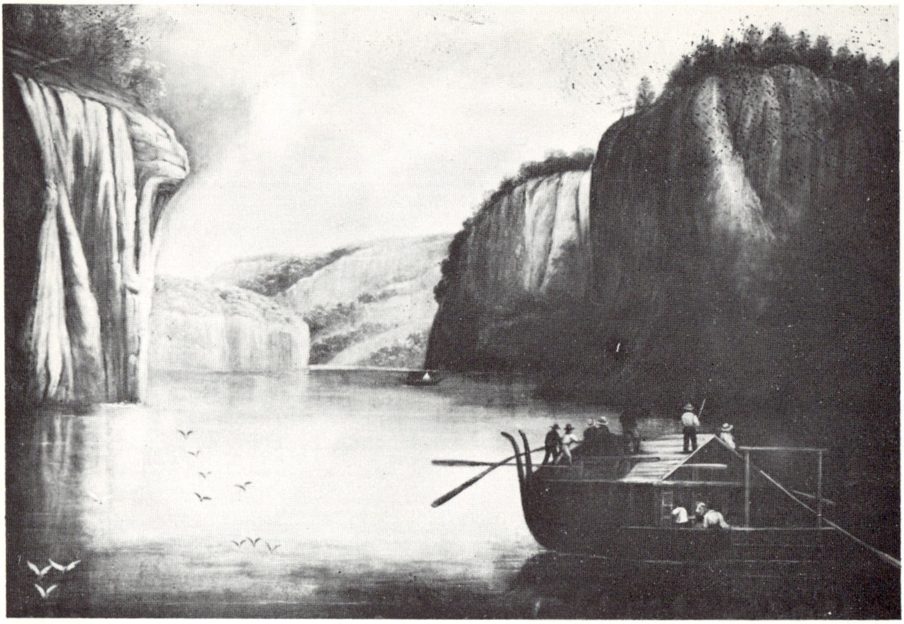

UNKNOWN PAINTER
Horn Boat on the Upper Mississippi; painted in a style similar to that used for painting the long Panoramas of the Mississippi, one of which was done by Pomarede (viz.).

New Orleans was approached from two directions; from down river by ocean traffic; and from up river by steamer and flat boat or the superior horn boat illustrated here, which was steered and propelled by a long sweep, as we understand it, mounted between the horns.

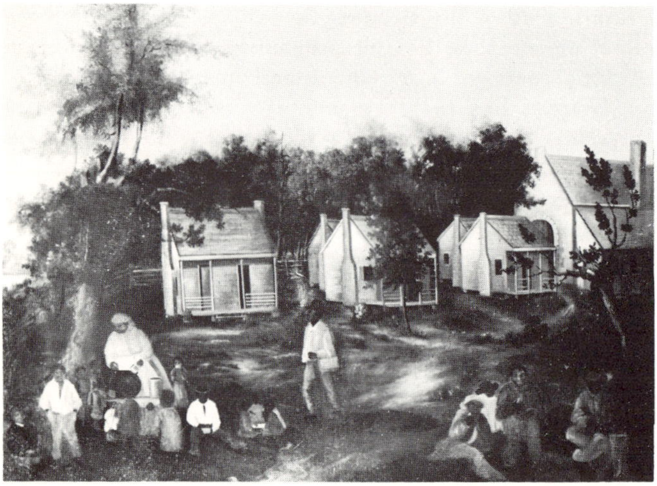

Primitive painting;
"Life on the Plantation"
29" x 36"

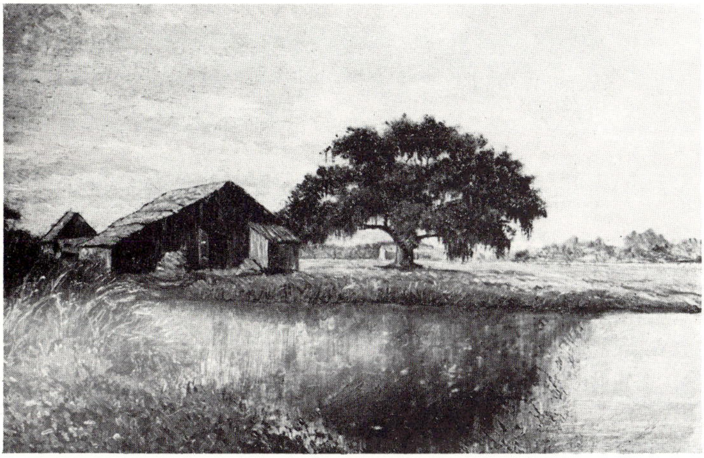

(A. Gamotis?)
"Barn on the Bayou"
11" x 16"

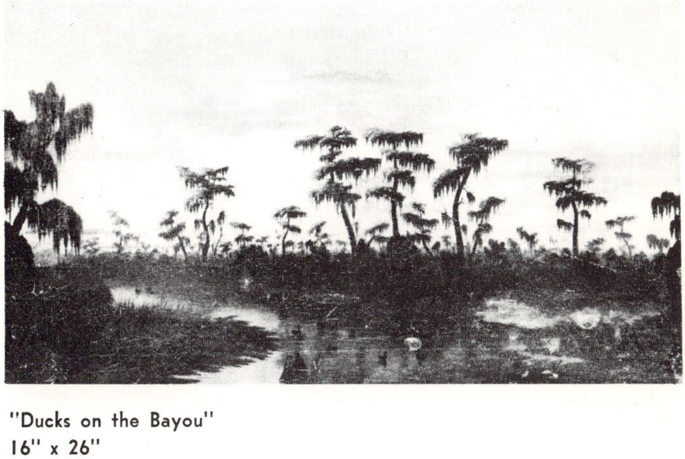

"Ducks on the Bayou"
16" x 26"

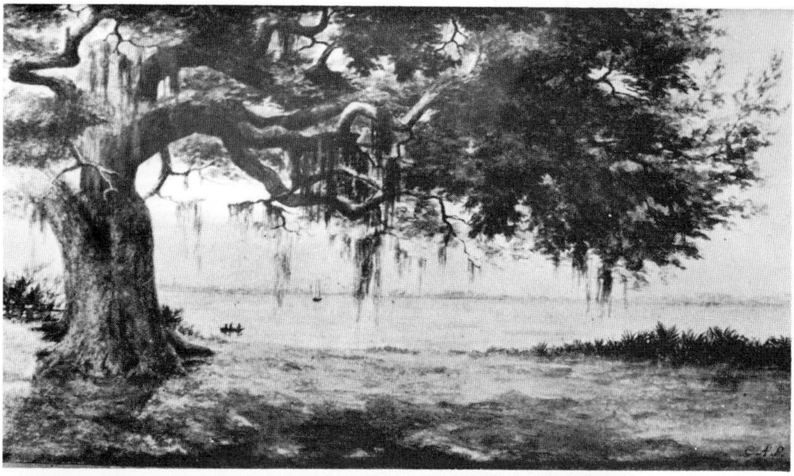

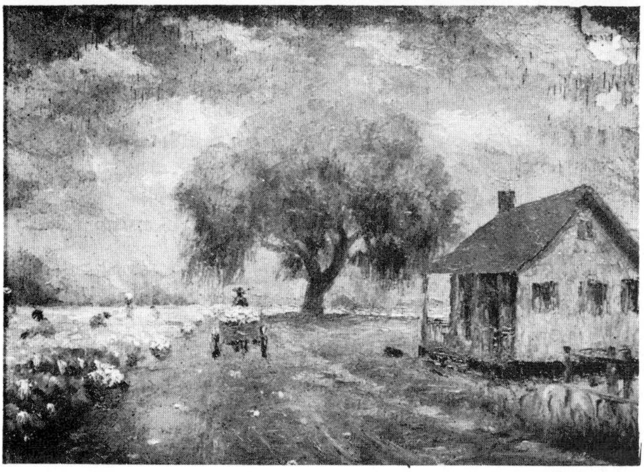

"Live Oak"
8" x 14"
Signed C.A.P.

"Cotton Harvest"
6" x 8"

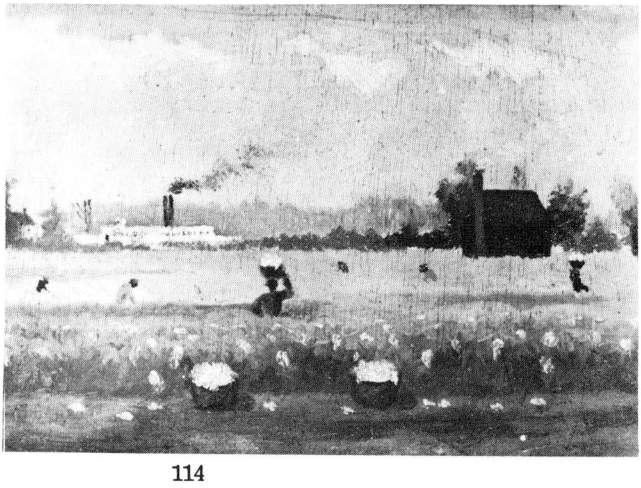

"Under the Levee"
6" x 8"

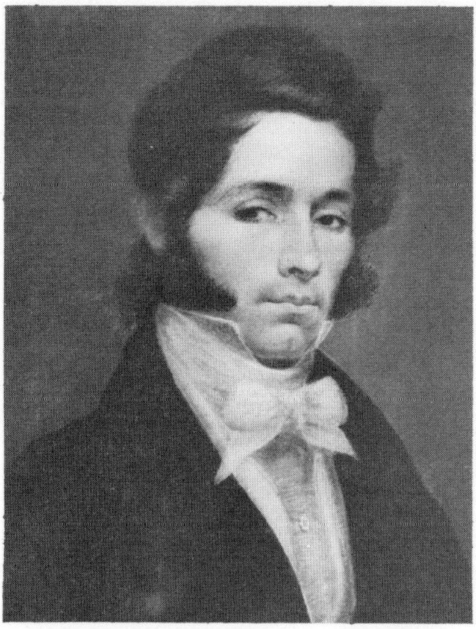

Portrait of Andrew Jackson's Flag Bearer "Stanislaus Nelson Peychaud", 20 1/4" x 16 1/8" Courtesy Isaac Delgado Mus. of Art, N. O. Gift of W. E. Groves

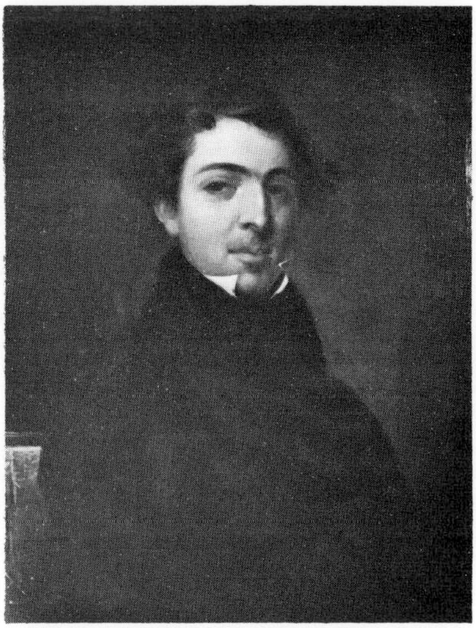

Portrait of Unknown Louisianian 29¼" x 24"

These two fine portraits are by one of the outstanding American painters. Inman, Vanderlyn, Morse and Jarvis all did portraits in Louisiana. We incline to a Morse attribution, particularly for the one on the right because of the hair treatment and elongated structure of collar and shoulders.

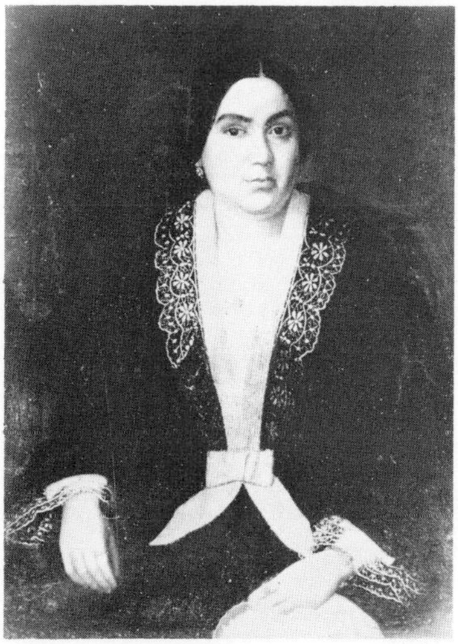

Portrait of Mrs. Beltram, duplicate of one in the La. State Mus. This one bears the inscription, "Hecho por Antonio Mart . . . (?) sordo". 32" x 25½"

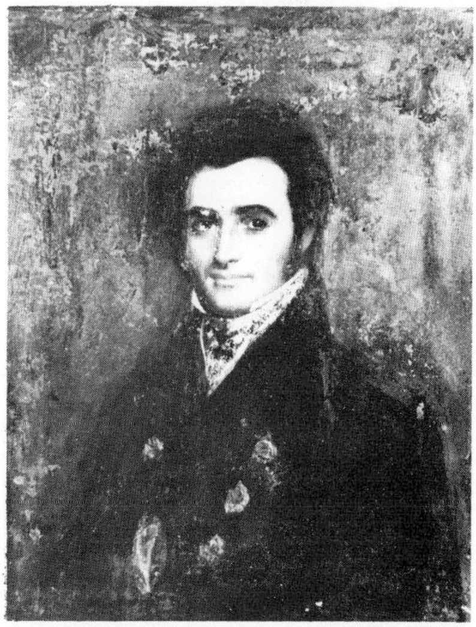

Portrait of Gen. Bossier of Natchitoches. A fine portrait formerly obscured by overpaint, now in process of restoration. 30" x 25"

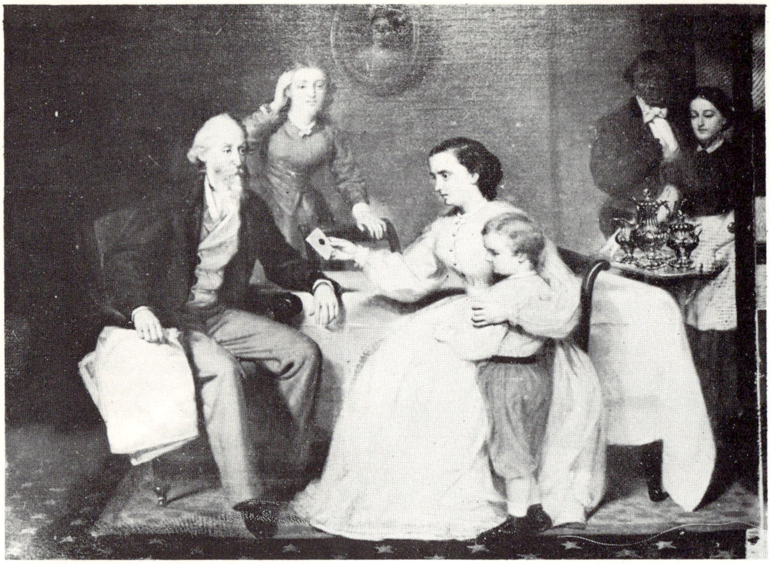

UNKNOWN ARTIST "Bad News" 21" x 26"

George A. Lambdin (1830-1896) is a possible attribution for this painting, if it was painted in the Louisiana-Mississippi area where it turned up. A similar family group exists in Natchez painted by him. He was the son of the portrait painter, James R. Lambdin. Both he and his father spent time in Natchez where they had close relatives, and portraits by both survive in the area.

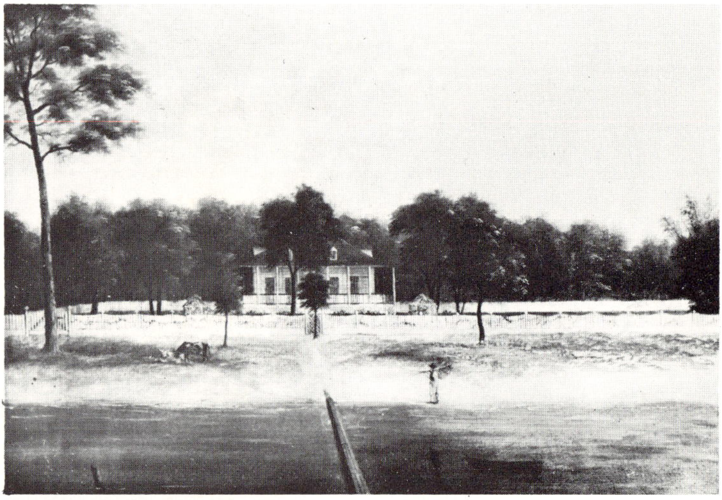

UNKNOWN ARTIST "Promised Land Plantation" 25" x 30"

"Promised Land" is one of the earliest houses surviving in Plaquemines Parish, situated on the east side of the Mississippi River below English Bend. It is presently owned by Mr. J. Ben Meyer, Sr., whose grandfather raised the house four feet when the levee was raised.

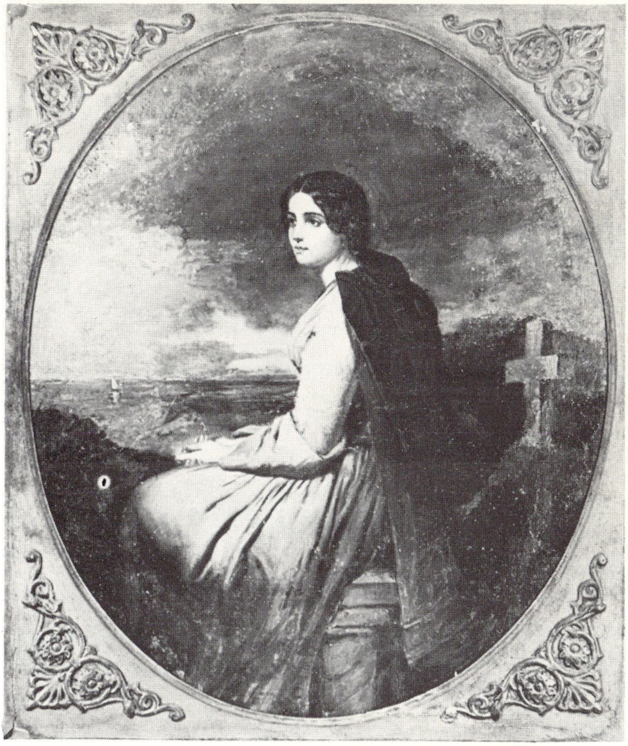

Partially restored

"Evangeline", by Thomas Faed, a Scotsman, was of course a favorite painting in Louisiana, the locale of the ending of this tragically romantic tale. Faed's painting was reproduced in an engraved cut to illustrate Longfellow's poem, and also in a print by Currier & Ives. Several copies of Faed's painting exist in Louisiana, of which this may be one, although it is fine enough to have been by Faed's own hand. It is reproduced here in its partly restored state and in the condition in which it was found by a bottle-hunter in the ruins of an old house in St. Bernard Parish. The dress is grey with a deep blue cloak and sunset afterglow in the sky. Faed's model was a Manchester working girl with undoubtedly no resemblance to the original of the Evangeline story, but for everyone now, this is Evangeline.

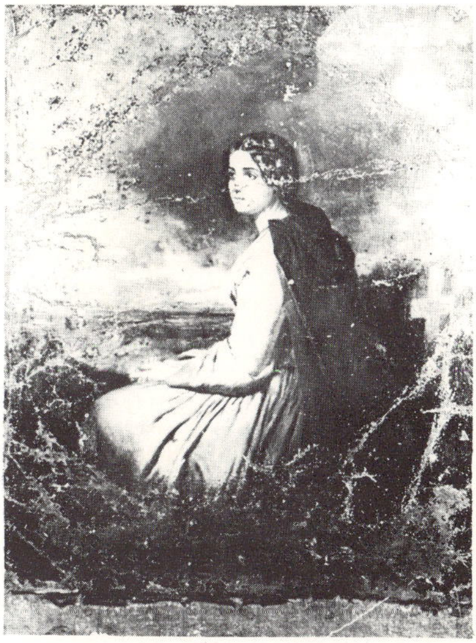

Before restoration

Cover Illustrations:

Viavant	Crawfish watercolor 11" x 6"
Julio	"Haw Yar" oil on canvas 32" x 43"